Mind Your Money, Girl!

A Self-Healing Approach to Hustle Less, Earn More Money, and Live Comfortably

Nan D. Ross

professional before attempting any techniques outlined in this book.

By reading this document, the reader agrees that under no circumstances is the author responsible for any losses, direct or indirect, that are incurred as a result of the use of the information contained within this document, including, but not limited to, errors, omissions, or inaccuracies.

Table of Contents

"All of life possibilities are inside of the mind. Therefore, mindfulness is the superpower to new money."

- Nan D. Ross

Introduction

We were led to believe it takes hard work, multiple jobs, or decades of savings to be prosperous. That's a lie! There is no shortage of money or time. When there's a focus of shortage, your perception of lack has strayed from your higher power. When you believe that hard work is what you need to do, then hard work you shall do. Financial success doesn't require hard work. It requires alignment of thoughts, emotions, and belief. Whatever, you need or want is already out there. Just "think" your way to a better life, and be ready to claim it.

Mind Your Money, Girl! is not about how to make money but how to shift your mindset from scarcity, and the financial challenges of money, to abundance perspective. The techniques in this book will help your brain re-create a new neural pathway to create a wealth mindset. Manifesting comes easily when there's no resistance or blocks. Money emotions and self-limited belief serve as a concrete wall that blocks one from manifesting abundance and wealth. As you pile away layers of harmful emotions and belief, the wall will come down.

Everything around us is a manifestation of energy. It takes energy for plants to grow, and when we eat them, we experience a burst of energy. It took energy for one sperm to swim faster than a million others and fertilize an egg so you could come into existence. It takes energy to lose weight and get into shape, energy to build and sustain long-lasting relationships, and energy to work diligently and succeed in your career.

If everything is a manifestation of energy, money is an energy too, and earning money or accumulating more of it requires a certain kind of energy. The problem I've seen in my social context, which I also speak about in my money healing course, is many people aren't aware of the many ways they are repelling money from them. You might say, "Oh, come on, Nan! Why would I repel something I desire so much?" I hear responses like these all the time, and I keep my answer short: You may desire money, but the energy you're putting out to the Universe tells a different story.

As a single mother, I know what it feels like to have all the bills pile up at the end of the month, not knowing where I'll find the money to pay them. I didn't become a single mother by choice. I divorced my first husband because I was tired of living miserably with an abusive partner. I had a second shot at love, but this ended in divorce too because I was with a man who didn't want to work and was happy to have me as the breadwinner.

After my divorce, I was emotionally free, but it took time for me to become financially liberated. From the outside, people saw a woman who was fearless and had everything put together, but no one sat with me in the middle of the night as I applied for short-term loans, just so I could make it through another month. I looked powerful because I was managing two jobs, but deep down I felt powerless because of the mounting debt and the guilt from not spending as much time as I could with my son.

I'm sure there are many single mothers who can relate to how I felt. Having to choose between feeding the family or paying household bills seems cruel and unfair. No one shares her daily responsibilities or helps her plan a prosperous financial future. Some single mothers are college graduates, yet their earnings don't reflect the full potential of their professional abilities. Single mothers also face the longest and highest unemployment rate when compared to similarly educated peers, and to make matters worse, many lack or receive very little financial support from the noncustodial parent or the government.

As a result of the financial pressures single mothers face, they often experience what I like to call blocked money emotions. When they think about money or receive an email or letter regarding their deteriorating finances, they may feel heaviness in their chest, tension in their neck and shoulder muscles, pulsating migraines, or emotional overwhelm. Sometimes, when triggered by past experience of unemployment or feeling financially insecure, these women may either feel helpless, react with rage, or emotionally withdraw.

Mind Your Money, Girl! is dedicated to all of the single mothers and female breadwinners who are committed to getting a grip on their finances and manifesting the abundant life they deserve. The book has been written in several parts and includes an exploratory process, how-to guide, and exercises and examples to help single mothers during their money healing journey. I will share stories and examples from my clients and students who have taken my money healing course and have experienced amazing results from shifting their money mentality. The four parts of this book include:

Part I: Identify the Money Blocks

Part II: Clear the Money Blocks

Part III: Reprogram the Mindset to Create a New Money Reality

Part IV: Plan for Passive and Multiple Streams of Income

As you perform the self-healing techniques offered in each part of the book, you will experience a shift of energy within the body. Some of my students have reported experiencing immediate relief, whereas others had to repeat the exercises for total relief. I strongly urge you to start from the beginning and work through every lesson in sequence. I also wouldn't recommend reading the entire book in one sitting because of the amount of focus most exercises demand. The best approach is to dedicate at least one week, per section, for learning and applying the techniques.

Mind Your Money, Girl! involves releasing and restoring energy, which may weigh heavily on your energy system. If you feel overwhelmed, take a moment to regulate your breathing, calm your mind, and spend time processing what you have already learned, rather than taking in new information.

Lastly, some of the exercises in this book have to be repeated based on the number of money stories or experiences that may be causing a blockage. Although going through one money block exercise on the first try can release that blockage, your most significant benefits will come through repetition. It's no different from learning a new skill, as repetition and hands-on training are the best ways to receive results.

As you embark on your money healing journey, synchronicity events will present themselves to you.

Here is a few I have experienced, and you may to:
- Job raises, bonus, or promotion
- New position making more money
- Unexpected money, gifts, and winnings
- Money for basic expenses such as rent, food, and utilities manifests
- Receive the last unemployment check when suddenly a job comes along
- Meet someone who presents a money-making opportunity

When you are ready, I invite you to begin your money awakening.

Part I:

Identify the Money Blocks

"I truly believe that women should be financially

independent from their men."

-Beyoncé

Chapter 1:

Money Is Just an Illusion

Perhaps the most important truth you need to know to heal your relationship with money is that money is a form of energy. You can think of money as being another form of consciousness, the same way you are. It is attracted to and repelled by things, just as you are attracted to and repelled by certain factors in your environment. When you begin to look at money in this way, you realize that money isn't difficult to earn or multiply. Suddenly, you stop putting money on a pedestal in your life and begin to look at it neutrally.

Since money is energy, it also enjoys being free to move. I know of many people who have a habit of hoarding money or clinging to it desperately when they have it. For them, it's a safe way to guarantee that the money stays in their bank account and over time grows. However, the nature of money is to ebb and flow. It enjoys being spent just as much as it is happy being multiplied (it usually does its best work when it's moving from one place or person to another).

Believe it or not, money desires to flow into your bank account. Its desire is to be useful in your life. The question, however, is how hospitable you have been over the years to money. Does money feel like your bank account is a safe place for it to multiply? Is it drawn to helping you accomplish your financial goals and live the lifestyle you can only dream of?

To assess where you stand with money, you would need to check your own energy. Your particular energy attracts things that are similar or of the same vibrational frequency as it. In other words, your relationship with money is determined by how you think, feel, and behave toward it. Whether you are aware of it or not, you are communicating hundreds of messages every day at an energetic frequency. These messages are a sum of what you believe to be true about yourself, your environment, your future, and your ability to live comfortably!

If most of your time is spent thinking about the possibility of going broke, you have made the possibility of going broke true for you. You have given birth to the thought that carries its own energetic frequency. With this thought comes a host of possible manifestations, like incurring more debt, losing your source of income, and other outcomes that seek to make "going broke" true in your life. What may look like life going against you may simply be the manifestations of your own energy that repel money and cause financial woes.

Your Perception of Money Becomes Your Reality

Our brain is consistently integrating information about our environment to make probabilistic decisions. Those decisions drive our sensory experience. Therefore, we have slightly different perceptions based on an experience. We can hear and see money differently. If we can see, think, and feel a different way using sensory perception, we can move away from what we believe as being false or untrue to what's true to ourselves.

Throughout this book and during the exercises, I will reference sensory perception. Sensory perception is processing the stimuli in our environment between the sense organs and the brain. Hearing, vision, taste, smell, and touch are the five senses we possess. Effective visualization involves using the five senses. Using the senses will increase manifesting power and multiply the results.

How diverse is your perception of money? Do you only see it with your eyes, located so far away that you cannot touch it with your hands or hear it piling up in your bank account? With every exercise you will be tasked with in this book, I will challenge you to increase your sensory perception of money by adjusting your past relationship with money and matching it with the frequency of success, winning, and abundance. After each exercise you will feel a greater connection and intimacy with money, and your senses will be on high alert, ready to see it, touch it, and hear it when it comes!

Good Vibes Attract Mo' Money

Have you ever heard people say, "You need to have a degree to make money" or "You need to know the right people to make money"? These assumptions imply that making money comes as a result of external outcomes. I once had a student who told me that for many years they believed they weren't destined to be successful because of the impoverished community they come from. They perceived their low social value as being a disqualifying factor in becoming successful. However, since money is a form of energy, anyone, regardless of where they come from, whether they have a degree or not or whether they are married or single, is eligible to attract money.

What qualifies you to attract money are your thoughts and emotions. These are the building blocks of your material world. What you think of and feel frequently is what ends up manifesting in your life. This is the foundation of the Law of Attraction. The chances of you attracting money when you feel guilty for the success you already have are slim. How can an energy as abundant be drawn to someone who feels guilty for having it?

When you begin regarding your thoughts as things, it will be easier for you to let go of limiting beliefs and entertain those that are aligned to your financial goals. For example, do you want financial struggles? Then don't entertain thoughts related to your lack. Later on in the book, I will show you how you can release stories of lack that you may have been harboring since childhood, but for now it's important to simply focus on what you want to see manifest in your life, not what you fear.

If you are short of positive things to think about, consider filling your mind with these thoughts:

1. I Am Worthy of Making Money

Being wealthy is my birthright. I was born to live a life of comfort. My bank account is the perfect recipient for money. My household is a magnet for financial success. I am worthy of financial breakthrough. All of my hard work is paying off. I attract money effortlessly, without any sacrifice. It is a joy to make money.

2. Making Money Is Possible

Making money comes easily to me. I am the perfect vibrational match for wealth. When money sees me, it feels safe to come to me. I know what I want, and the Universe is rewarding me for it. There are so many opportunities to make money all around me. I have so many channels of wealth open to me. Anything is possible.

3.   I Am Grateful for What I Already Have

I am grateful for the roof over my head. I am fortunate to have a car that moves me from point A to point B. The access to the Internet has opened up so many opportunities for me. I am blessed to have a job that pays all of my bills. I receive so much support and encouragement from my family and friends. I am living an abundant life. All of my needs are met.

Exercise: Reliving Your Accomplishments

The purpose of this exercise is to help you understand how your body responds when you have a great sense of success or accomplishment. Instead of talking about it, you will learn how to feel the emotions of success.

Begin by recalling a memory when you had a feeling of a financial accomplishment. It could've been landing a new job, receiving a promotion at work, purchasing a house or car, or even winning a scratch-off ticket. Regardless of what it may have been, select a memory that left a huge impression on you and made you feel proud of yourself.

As you begin to reminisce, recall the experience from a first-person perspective. To do this you can think of the memory from an "I" perspective. What positive feelings are you reexperiencing? Can you remember your facial expressions? Are you currently smiling as you relive the experience?

What type of sensations do you feel within your body? Are you feeling chills, a flow of dynamic energy, or sense of openness? Whatever positive feeling you're experiencing, pay attention to the location of the feeling. Where do you feel the sense of ease? Is it in your chest, head, legs, back, or somewhere else?

Practicing this exercise proves how valuable this book can be for you. When you apply this technique to your life, you are actively deciding how you want to feel toward any financial challenge or setback. Later in the book, you will begin to include other stimuli, such as pictures, sounds, taste, and touch.

Chapter 2:

Money Is About Your Emotions

No one is always rational when making financial decisions. Yes, we would all like to believe we are because we're adults, right? But if we look at where our money goes and how much of it we save, we will see that many of our money decisions are based on emotion.

I'll never forget working with a client who had bought herself a brand-new Mercedes-Benz because she wanted to prove to her family that she was "making it" in life. The upfront deposit of the car was something she could afford, but paying the monthly car installments proved to be a nightmare. Her decision to purchase the car was based on a bitter feeling she had toward her family. Perhaps if she had processed how she felt toward her family, she would've picked a reasonably priced car within her budget.

In the first chapter, we spoke about money being an energy. The spiritual aspect of money is a theme that I will refer to many times throughout the book. However, there is also a psychological aspect of money that is also worth understanding. For a moment, think about money as being something you have a complicated relationship with. The way you interact with and manage money has a direct relation to how you feel about money and how it makes you feel about yourself.

The most potent emotions in relation to money are shame, fear, guilt, and envy. To figure out how many people's relationship with money gets to this point, we would need to work backward. For instance, we would need to look at how the person interacts with or manages their money. Someone feeling guilt toward money is probably a money hoarder and doesn't allow it to flow in and out of their life. A person who feels envy toward money will probably purchase goods they can't afford just to impress their followers on social media.

When I learned that I had an unhealthy attachment with money, it was liberating. My behavior toward budgeting my finances finally made sense. I was so scared of the possibility of going broke or being evicted from our home that I put money on a pedestal. I was obsessed with the price of things, and whenever I would swipe my card, I would cringe. I was both fearful of losing money and making money, and this behavior wasn't taking me anywhere.

Being aware of my emotions in relation to money brought much needed awareness in my financial affairs. It allowed me to pause and think: What am I really afraid of? I could think of a hundred scenarios to be fearful of, but when I thought back on each one, they were all scenarios that were based on emotions, not facts. For instance, I was fearful of seeing a late rent notice taped on my door, and thinking one day they would kick me and my son out. The fact of the matter is I had always paid my rent on time, and my job was secure enough to ensure I would be able to make rent payments consistently, every month.

Emotional Impulse Drives Money Decisions

When you are not aware of your emotional states and how they influence your money decisions, you can easily fall into the trap of emotional spending. Emotional spending occurs when your emotional state triggers impulse buying. It can be as simple and uncomplicated as buying yourself a tub of ice cream because you feel stressed or as complicated as binding yourself to a loan so you can redecorate your home to make it look like something straight out of a catalogue.

There are a number of emotions that can influence your purchasing decisions. I have written down a few below. As you go through each one, think about the last time you made a financial decision based on these emotions.

Loneliness: Many people turn to shopping when they are feeling lonely. For some reason, filling our refrigerators, closets, or homes with more stuff can cheer us up when we're feeling sad.

Boredom: Internet shopping has become the miracle cure for boredom. Never has it been this easy to click and add items to a shopping cart. Whether you are shopping for gadgets, books, cosmetics, or accessories, Google has a directory of online stores that you can spend many hours scrolling through.

Stress: There are some people who won't spend a cent when they are stressed because spending money contributes to their sense of being out of control. However, there are also some who spend a lot of money frivolously when stressed, as a way to escape the present uncomfortable feelings.

Jealousy: A jealous person will purchase something they don't need because someone else has it. They will often feel incompetent when they don't have what others do. This unhealthy competition causes them to take out loans or overspend on their credit cards to keep up with other people's wallets and budgets.

Excitement: Many times, when we're excited about a new idea or plan, we will want to celebrate it. Celebrating small or big victories is a way for us to express our happiness or gratitude. For example, if you have received a raise at work, you might feel an urge to take your family on trips or redo the interior of your house. The feeling of excitement compels many people to spend money they haven't budgeted for.

If you are an emotional spender looking for a way out, you will need to spend time looking in. Identify your emotional triggers that cause you to reach for your wallet or purchase items you don't need online. In those moments of spending, what feelings arise within you? Are you anxious, lonely, or frustrated? If so, delay your purchase for a few days and process the strong emotions you are feeling. Where does this emotion come from? What thought or experience triggered it? When you have processed the strong emotion, look back at your shopping cart and answer the following questions:

1. Why am I buying this?
2. Is this something I need right now?
3. Can I put the money to purchase this item to better use?
4. Can I delay this purchase for another week?

The Power of Money Anchors

The biggest difference between someone with money and someone without money is that the former has a lot more choices available to them than the latter. The more choices available to you, the greater the amount of freedom you can feel in your everyday life! Think about it this way: Someone who has money doesn't feel anxious paying their bills at the end of the month. In fact, they might not even notice automatic payments that go off on their bank accounts. However, someone who doesn't have a lot of money coming in is aware of every cent the bank comes to take, and they may feel a lot more stressed near the end of the month.

Being financially insecure does more damage on your psyche than it does to your credit score. For example, when you borrow money, you fall into debt, and this can lead to a low self-esteem, chronic stress, feelings of hopelessness, and impaired cognitive function (this is what makes getting out of the dark hole of debt seem impossible). Falling into debt can also cause what is known as debt denial, which is the act of dissociating from your current financial situation and ignoring the mounting debt. People who experience debt denial typically avoid answering phone calls that they suspect are coming from a debt collection agency, they underestimate how much they owe, or they leave bills unopened or throw them away.

When I was late on paying a bill, I used to avoid taking calls from the collection agency or I would ignore their past due bills. Seeing their number appear on my phone would instantly change my mood. I could've been in a lively mood and feeling optimistic about life, but as soon as I would get that phone call, my mood would change from jovial to anxious. Later on, I learned the reason this was happening was that I had unintentionally created an anchor.

An anchor is anything that reminds you of something. It can be a sound, logo, color, smell, taste, or touch. For instance, the sound of someone's voice or a symbol that reminds you of your childhood can trigger a memory. These anchors can influence how you react to life situations and if not changed, they can stay in your memory for years. My anchor was the bill collector phone number, and every time I saw that number I would react in a negative way. Not only would my mood change, I would also feel tension in my gut and sometimes my head.

Recognizing my anchor helped me change the way I responded to it. For instance, every time the collection agency called, I would think, "They want to help me sort out my financial affairs." This made me more willing to pick up the call and listen to what they had to say. It also made me less defensive on the line and a lot more open to receiving instruction on what I needed to do to improve my financial situation.

Exercise: Creating a Money Anchor

The purpose of this exercise is to create a touch anchor that you can use on yourself to trigger positive feelings while going through a financial challenge or setback. This anchor will give you a dose of love and success and it can be done at any time or any place, as long as it is in a discreet manner.

Open your nondominant hand with your palm facing down. If you are right-handed, you would open your left hand. Take your thumb and point finger from the other hand, and squeeze between your nondominant hand, between the thumb and point finger. You can add some pressure but not too much that it becomes painful. Continue to squeeze between your thumb and point finger; this will be your anchor for this exercise.

Close your eyes and recall a positive feeling or memory from the Reliving Your Accomplishment exercise. As you reminisce, slow the scene as if you're watching a movie, frame-by-frame. Go inside of the memory and relive it.

As you continue to replay the scene, try to remember your surroundings. Are you indoors or outdoors? What do you see in the background? What clothing are you wearing?

Keep replaying the scene from start to finish for another minute. Intensify the positive feelings by imaging how you were feeling at the time, and what your body language communicated. As you get to the peak of this "feel good" movie, squeeze between your thumb and point finger once more.

Now, I would like for you to find another positive feeling memory. This time it's a memory of getting something you have always wanted or that you love so much. It can be a person, place, or thing. Whatever it is, you must love it and it has to be better than the first memory from the Reliving Your Accomplishment exercise.

Think of that memory and recall an interaction with another person. You may just see a still photo of the memory or you may be watching yourself as a character in the movie. Nonetheless, immerse yourself in the experience and see it from your eyes (first-person perspective). Use your imagination and your five senses to amplify the feeling. Is there a particular aroma or fragrance in the air? What does the person you are interacting with look like? Can you touch them? Make the feeling twice or three times as strong as the first memory.

When you reach the peak of the positive feeling, squeeze between your thumb and point finger twice.

Imagine the euphoric feeling increasing even more. As the feeling increases, you may experience a good sensation swirling in your body. This is a good sign. Once again, squeeze between your thumb and point finger two more times.

Stop squeezing your hand and open your eyes. Take four deep breaths and come back to a normal state. Slowly count backward from 10 to one.

Finally, without recalling or reminiscing, squeeze between the thumb and point finger. Do you notice any good feelings that this action triggers?

Awesome job!

Chapter 3:

Stories Influence Your Money

Relationship

I was raised in a lower-middle-class neighborhood in Long Island, New York. My parents raising six children were able to provide us with the best; we always had the latest appliances and gadgets, yearly trips to Disney World and Miami, and ate at the best restaurants. This may seem like no big deal now, but we were the first family in the neighborhood to own a microwave oven in the early '80s. In these modern times, I would compare it to being the first family on the block to have a parked Mercedes-Benz on your driveway.

But this was only half of the picture (the half that all of the neighbors saw). What no one knew is how we would go from having a lot of disposable income one month to collecting coins and putting them together so we could buy bread and other essentials. Shocking, huh? The truth is there are many families across

America who live this double money life, living a lavish lifestyle that isn't sustainable.

For many years I couldn't explain the juxtaposition of the lifestyle we lived. Yes, everyone would watch us come back from a fancy restaurant with plastics full of takeaways, but no one would see me making my mom grilled cheese sandwiches with the thick slices of the government cheese (the best grilled cheese ever, by the way!). No one saw us get free and reduced lunch in school or having to use candles because my dad couldn't afford to pay the utility bills. I vividly remember a time when we didn't have heat so we had to boil pots of water to bathe. My siblings and I would fight over the stainless-steel pot of boiling water because none of us wanted to wait another 45 minutes for water to boil.

We lived this double money life because my father, although he was a good provider and my role model, wasn't a good saver. When he got money, he wanted to make my mother happy and buy her what she wanted.

I didn't think my upbringing and early exposure to money would have a significant impact on me. I guess I was wrong! The financial trauma from my childhood "conveniently" hit when I was married. I had married someone who wasn't big on saving and didn't think about finances practically. I became the triggered little girl who felt insecure about our family's financial situation and so I started to control all of our finances. This weighed a toll on me—and on our relationship— and I realized that besides marrying someone who resembled my father's money mindset, I desperately needed to heal from the experiences I had faced in childhood that were influencing my relationship with money as an adult.

Your Money Reality Is All in Your Head

You're probably thinking that certain people, cultural, and ethnic groups share the same money problems and struggles. This is far from the truth! For example, not all single mothers struggle financially. Not all people who drive luxury cars are rich. The relationship we have with others, how we feel about them, and how you feel about yourself are just filters that were created unintentionally.

What you believe about money has more to do with the filters you have created about the money.

Sheila grew up in an impoverished, crime-ridden community. She would often overhear the fights her parents had about money. She didn't understand why her family had to go without food on some nights, struggle to pay bills, or not have enough money to buy warm clothes. Needless to say, Sheila was traumatized by her parents' financial woes and grew up believing that life was unfair and people from her community were destined to live in poverty and earn minimum wages. Sheila's unresolved attitude and mindset toward money caused her to accept the first job she could find and never aim to grow in her career or achieve anything more than what her father could.

Next door to Sheila's house lived Kendra. Kendra was the same age as Sheila and came from a similarly poverty-stricken home environment. The girls would often share experiences about their financial struggles, and each one could relate with what the other was going through. However, Kendra was different because of how she viewed money. For her, money came with good ideas. She believed that growing up in an impoverished community gave her insight into solutions that could benefit the poor, and this led her to develop several business plans with several fundable ideas.

Since she didn't have money to fund his innovations or access to the funders, Kendra focused on excelling at school so that she could qualify for scholarships into the universities her parents couldn't afford to take her. Once again, this brilliant idea was based on Kendra's money mindset: money comes with good ideas. She was able to qualify for a full scholarship studying toward a finance degree, and while completing her degree, she found an angel investor. Within a few years, Kendra had built a successful startup and managed to move her entire family out of that impoverished community.

Both Sheila and Kendra were born and bred in the same environment and were exposed to the same resources. However, Kendra was able to go from ragsto-riches while Sheila became a statistic. Was it because Kendra was smarter than Sheila? No. She wasn't any more gifted than Sheila was, although she saw money differently.

My "Aha" Moment

The stories you tell yourself about your life can influence your ability to succeed. For instance, if you honestly believe that because of your skin color, certain opportunities are closed for you, you will always feel like your options to make money are slim to none. Alternatively, if you feel like because of your gender, many people will reject your business proposals, you may feel discouraged to knock on some doors, send 100 emails, or take risks outside of your comfort zone.

The old story I had about my life was downright miserable. I thought my life was turned upside-down when I went from being a stay-at-home married mother to a single working mother. I pitied myself and affirmed my fears more than I affirmed my strengths or ideas. For decades, I was worn out and had a "Do not mess with me" attitude. I wonder how many opportunities I missed because I simply didn't want to be bothered.

I was frustrated at the responsibility of being a provider, but equally frustrated at being close to bankruptcy. I was moody, burned-out, and resentful that I had no emergency fund, no financial support, and no emotional support. Oh and to top it all off, I hated my job! I used up all of my sick leaves so I had no more excuses for missing work. Since I was working full days, I had to pay for expensive childcare and extracurricular activities that burned holes in my wallet.

Just by sharing my old story, I'm sure you can sense how gloomy and depressed I felt. On an energetic level, this was the kind of message I was putting out into the Universe. Since like energy attracts like energy, what I was receiving from the Universe was subpar. By constantly complaining about my financial struggles, I was actually making them worse.

Oops!

Exercise: What Is Your Money Story?

Take a moment and think about your money story. What is your earliest memory of hearing about money and how was it spoken about? What were some of your childhood beliefs about money and where did you learn these beliefs? Are there any significant events that took place in your life that impacted how you grew up seeing money?

After taking time to reflect on your story, take a piece of paper and write down five beliefs you hold about money.

To access the PDF version of this worksheet visit: nandaleross.com/mind-your-money-girl-book/.

Exercise: What's Your Parents' Money Story?

After completing the first exercise, think about the ways in which your parents handled their finances. From the best of your knowledge, what kind of relationship did they have with money? If you grew up with both parents, which one was in charge of the finances, and how did this play out in their relationship? What are some of the phrases your parents used to repeat about money?

Here is my parents' money story:

I remember when my mother used phrases like "We're broke" or "We're poor." Most of the time when she would say these phrases, she would be crying. But after revisiting the memory in my head, I recall another memory when we got back from a Disney World trip. I don't know of any poor people who took annual family trips outside of the state, let alone to Disney World. I woke up with an epiphany: My parents were never broke or poor. They just didn't know how to manage their finances.

After taking the time to reflect on your parents' money story, on the same piece of paper, write down five things your parents taught you about money.

To access the PDF version of this worksheet visit: nandaleross.com/mind-your-money-girl-book/.

Exercise: What's Your Partner's Money Story?

The money beliefs that came as a result of your early childhood conditioning play a big role in your money relationship. However, when you form a partnership, whether it be a marriage, committed relationship, or business, you will start to unconsciously pick up on your partner's money stories. For instance, you will notice their food purchasing habits, liquor consumption, or how they prefer to buy a gram of weed rather than paying the power company.

Their story may sound like this:

Baby, I will reconnect the power when I get paid next week. Let us just relax, get some beer, and burn some candles. You want to play dominoes?

There are some partners who have no issues with:

- Sharing their neighbor's electricity
- Eating from the dollar menu

- Letting you down when they make excuses for not paying child support
- Piggy-backing off of you and your financial ambitions
- Showing interest in get-rich-quick schemes rather than putting in the work to earn their money
- Gambling their monthly salary or spending it on alcohol

Living with someone with toxic money habits can be challenging. You start to feel as if you're babysitting a grown person. This can be financially strenuous on you and your children, especially when your partner doesn't consistently contribute to the household bills.

When I reflect upon my ex's money story, all I can say is this: A man can't be crowned king without demonstrating kingly qualities.

Take a moment and reflect on your partner's money story. It doesn't have to be your romantic partner; it can be your business partner too. Write down what you believe their money story is, and assess how similar or different it is from yours.

To access the PDF version of this worksheet visit: nandaleross.com/mind-your-money-girl-book/.

Exercise: Dissociating From Your Money Story

If you were paying close attention, in the last two exercises, you may have noticed I used the terms such as "be immersed in the experience" or "relive the experience." This is known as "associating with the experience." Since some of our money stories may be unpleasant, in this exercise, you will practice disassociation, which is observing yourself (in the third person) as you relive the memory or looking at yourself from a distance. It's like watching yourself playing a character in a movie.

To begin, pick one of the money stories, between your parents, partner, or yourself. The money story will be a scene in a movie. As you recall the memory, imagine you're watching the scene play out on a big screen, frame by frame.

Recall what you see happening. Who was there? Describe the background? What were the other people wearing? How were they feeling? Were they upset, sad, angry? How were you feeling? What were you doing? What was your body language?

Continue to replay the scene from start to finish. When you replay the scene again, imagine the scene turning from color to black and white. Continue to replay the scene for another 30 seconds.

Imagine the scene turning from black and white to fuzzy. If you can still see the scene, replay until the entire movie is fuzzy and unrecognizable.

Open your eyes and come back to the present moment. Take four deep breaths, and come back to a normal state. Slowly count backward from 10 to one.

Just as a reminder for the upcoming exercises, when you need to recall money worries or stressful memories, use the dissociate method. This will help you analyze the situation from an observer's perspective without feeling like you are stepping back into time and reliving the intense negative emotions firsthand. When you recall a pleasant memory, you can use the associate method (placing yourself inside the memory) to intensify the positive emotions.

Chapter 4:

Money Gossip

A 2011 study that was published by the *Journal of Financial Therapy* measured the reactions of 422 people to 72 money-related beliefs or statements (Erb Financial, 2013). Examples of the kind of statements reviewed, include:

- Poor people are lazy.
- It's not polite to speak about money.
- Things will get better when I have more money.
- There is virtue living with less money.

Based on the findings, financial psychologist Brad Klontz and colleagues were able to identify four main money scripts that influenced how the respondents viewed money. For the most part, these money scripts are unconscious beliefs that people carry from childhood, which end up driving their financial behaviors as adults.

The Four Gossip Groups

These four money scripts can also be seen as four gossip groups. Why gossip groups? Because in general, everyone in a gossip group speaks the same language. As you grow through each money gossip group, identify which language you relate to you most. You may also be able to identify gossip groups that your friends, family members, or partner fits into.

1. "Money Is Bad" Gossip Group

This group thinks money is bad or they are unworthy or undeserving of money. This belief consists of behaviors like financial denial or financial rejection. This group is known to ignore their budget, abuse their credit, avoid asking for a raise, or avoid opening their bills. The demographic characteristics linked to this group is more likely to be young (between the age of 18 and 30), and single, less educated, and less wealthy.

Typical Money Story:

Money is evil. It changes people and causes some to either abandon their families or make bad decisions. Wealthy people are the epitome of greed. How can one person have so much money? Are they planning on taking that money to the grave? Ugh. I'm actually disgusted by people who make financial success a goal. Why can't they be satisfied with the little they have? I mean, as long as someone has a job and pays their bills, they can live happily, right?

2. "Money Is Power" Gossip Group

This group believes money is about status, and someone's self-worth is measured by their net worth. Money and luxury brand symbols are important to them. This group is overly concerned about success and materialism. These are the individuals who wear luxury brand names but ignore their budget, overspend, are attracted by get-rich-quick schemes, and obsessed about raising their social status. They avoid asking for a raise or avoid opening their bills. The demographic characteristics linked to this group are more likely to be young, single, less educated, and less wealthy.

Typical Money Story:

I am obsessed with money. I believe that money makes the world go around and without money, humans are useless. I like to surround myself with wealthy people who smell like money. They make me feel powerful and important. I won't be seen in public with people who look broke or who have financial struggles. Quite frankly, those types of people need to live on a separate planet. There's no such thing as too much money, unless you think too much happiness is a bad thing. I shop a lot and only buy the finest things. I deserve to live a life of luxury.

3. "Money Makes Life Better" Gossip Group

This group thinks that if they can increase their income or receive a financial windfall, they would solve all of their problems This belief can be associated with money disorders such as pathological gambling, workaholism, compulsive hoarding, or buying and overspending. The demographic characteristics linked to this group includes being young, white, and single and having lower levels of income and net worth.

Typical Money Story:

Wealthy people earn their respect. Without money, a person doesn't have any influence or power. Money can buy you friends, open doors you couldn't previously access, and get you inside the VIP section of a party. I believe in the philosophy of "fake it till you make it," because unless you show an image of having money, no one will pay attention to you. I have to win people's love and honor by making as much money as I can, even if I have to lie or cheat my way to the top.

4. "Money Makes Me Uncomfortable" Gossip Group

This group believes money is a deep form of shame, especially those who are ashamed of having too much or too little money. Sometimes someone gets to a certain age, and they feel they should have done better financially. This group also believes the topic of money should be secrecy. This group hides their money under a mattress. This group considered money to be taboo and a sensitive topic to share with friends, family, and the world.

In a survey 40% percent say it's acceptable to keep financial secrets from their spouse, and 40% of married respondents admit they told their spouse they spent less on a purchase than they did (Hogan, 2020).

My parents sold a house they had in Long Island and got paid cash at closing. My dad wanted to purchase a brand-new Mercedes, but my mother told him it wasn't a good idea. It wasn't that they couldn't afford it, but my mother didn't want to show people how much money we had. She said, "People in the congregation would be jealous if we buy a Mercedes." My dad has held on to that grudge for more than 30 years.

I believe we should be far more open with our financial situation. Now, I'm not saying to go and tell people how much your salary is (this is one of the most personal questions you can ever ask someone). What you do with your money is your business. But if we keep our financial situation a secret, we will continue to feel isolated and ashamed of our financial situations.

Typical Money Story

Money doesn't grow on trees; once you've spent it, there's no telling when you will make it up again. Counting each penny is the best way to grow wealth. Try to spend as little as you can and put the rest in savings. My biggest fear is going broke or not being able to afford my lifestyle. This is why I'm cautious in how I spend my money. I keep up-to-date with my taxes and student loan debt because I don't want to get in trouble with the federal government.

Chapter 5:

Down-Low Dirty Money

Secrets

I fell into the financial trap of keeping quiet about my finances. In 2016, I got heavily into the Law of Attraction and manifestation, and even after teaching and publishing dozens of videos with scientific proof that our thoughts create our reality, friends and family didn't take me seriously. Most thought I was crazy and living a fantasy life built on whimsical theories. They would say, "If you're such a great manifestor, why are you still driving a Ford Fusion? Why do you still have a prepaid cell phone? Why are you still renting? Why are you not wearing name brands? Ugh! Why do you live in that neighborhood?"

All the while in judgment they were hiding a big secret: They were heavily in debt.

They pretended they had less debt than I did. They spent more on clothes and entertainment than I could afford and would pick up rounds of drinks for friends and only bought top-notch liquor (instead of hosting a few friends at home). I guess they were fearful that "others" would think they didn't make enough money and so they were willing to keep this secret hidden for as long as possible. It got to the point where it was difficult to keep up, and they had to wake up to their grim reality.

The Moment of Truth

Don't get me wrong, I'm not perfect, and I had to face the consequences of my own dirty money secrets. The consequences were that I was deeper in debt than I ever was before. Instead of beating myself up about it, I used it as a teachable moment. I learned that it's better to live a life that looks basic than to pretend to be someone you're not and have to live an expensive double life.

I know I'm not the only person in the world who has kept a dirty money secret. There are so many people who are disguising the truth about their situation and suffering because of it. To those people, I would like to say, Don't be afraid of your financial situation, no matter how much people tease you about it or how humiliating it is. Some day your truth will evolve, and you will be living a completely different life, a life that matches the visions in your dreams.

However, before you can attain that kind of life, you need to speak your truth. Be honest about your financial situation and how fearful you are about it. Think about your money story and beliefs, and figure out where they come from. The only way to move forward is by confronting the barriers of self-limiting beliefs that stand in front of you. You can overcome these self-limiting beliefs by slaying them one at a time.

While we're on the subject of truth, here are a few self-limiting beliefs that are cancerous to your financial future:

1. **"I'm going to run out of money and be destitute."**

Money secret: I feel financially insecure.

This money belief affects your sense of survival, stability, and security. It causes you to feel incapable or unworthy of making money consistently and feeling safe and secure. This belief is driven with fear-based thoughts that can lead to debt, money struggles, guilt, greed, and obsession with material goods and money.

Emotional Challenge: Overcoming the fear, guilt, or anxiety related to making money.

2. **"I'm not smart enough to make that kind of money."**

Money secret: I undermine my own ability to provide for myself.

This belief affects your sense of willpower, self-esteem, and confidence. It's the inability to take actions to make enough money or bring financial dreams into reality due. This belief manifests into low-self-esteem and self-criticism. It holds you back from finding out what it takes to start a side-hustle and believe in yourself, because you said, "I don't know how to do it." Instead of researching or seeking advice, you watch time pass without making any effort to pursue your dreams.

Emotional Challenge: Overcoming past disappointment, doubts, and failures that may be making you fearful of taking on new opportunities.

3. "I'm jealous of someone else's success, passion, and creativity."

Money secret: I don't believe in my own ability to make money.

This money belief affects your sense of desire, passion, and creativity to create your financial success without competition. It's the inability to find the passion to pursue your financial freedom. Most people will not admit to being jealous of someone's success. Instead, they may say or think, "They think they are all that." Or, they would unfriend a follower because they are posting pictures of them enjoying their lifestyle. This belief leads to gossip and being judgmental of others, finding information to downplay someone's credibility or success.

Emotional Challenge: Overcoming the worry of one day becoming financially free.

Exercise: Rate Your Emotional Wealth

Let us try this exercise together.

We have to learn how to identify negative feelings before we can resolve them.

In this quick exercise, I want you to understand how your body feels or reacts when you express certain feelings:

- Think of someone; a neighbor, or a family member who you think is doing well financially. Think of a material possession that they have achieved that you want, whether it may be a car, a big house, or the like.
- Visualize that person engaging with their material possession (driving their car, going on vacation, etc.).
- Hold the vision for 60 seconds.
- Become aware of any tension, emotions, or the feeling of heaviness in your body.
- If you do not feel pressure, describe what you feel as you hold the vision.
- Now let's repeat the process.

- Think of that person engaging with their abundance.
- Instead, you will transform the contracted emotions (jealousy, anger, envy) by sending them the energy of happiness. You can send "I'm happy for you" energy.
- Remember, you are six degrees of separation from your connections, including your neighbors, friends, and even mutual friends on social media. If they got it, you can get it too.
- Hold the vision for 60 seconds while smiling to yourself. Smiling releases feel-good hormones and reduces the stress level.
- How do you feel? Do you notice the energy expands?

Have you noticed how your energy responds to your thoughts?

To access the meditation version of this exercise visit: nandaleross.com/mind-your-money-girl-book/.

Self-Limiting Money Beliefs, Continued

So far, what have you learned about self-limiting money beliefs? Have you noticed how they are always hiding a deeper need or an area in your life in which you feel a sense of lack? Holding on to self-limiting money beliefs may feel comfortable in the short-term, but as soon as you resolve the underlying fear, doubt, or lack, the self-limiting money belief will become a false assumption.

As you work through your self-limiting money beliefs, imagine them as false assumptions about who you are and what you are capable of. Below is a list of a few more self-limiting money beliefs. As you go through each one, stop for a moment and recognize them as being false assumptions of the past, present, or the future.

"If I charge more they won't pay for my services."

This belief shows a lack of being compensated for my efforts or not making enough money.

"I'm going to run out of money and be poor or homeless."

This belief is the lack of security and stability. It's the inability to make money consistently and to feel safe and secure.

"I can't save enough money."

This belief shows the lack of confidence to manage money.

"I can't do this on my own."

This belief shows the lack of confidence in becoming financially independent and a lack of willpower to take action to make money or bring dreams into reality.

"I'm not appreciated by those close to me."

This belief shows the lack of worthiness, fear of rejection, and the need to be loved. This belief shows an inability to enjoy the fruits of your labors with your children, family, and friends.

"I don't trust people with my money."

This belief shows a lack of trust in dealing with people around your money. It's the fear that money will be taken away from you. If you have experienced this already, I understand how the belief can be a safety blanket—I was scammed out of thousands of dollars, twice.

"I'm afraid to speak my truth because I will be judged."

This belief speaks to the fear of creative expression and judgment. I have women clients and students who tell me they would love to blog, create videos or audio podcasts related to their true passion, but they are afraid of criticism.

"It's too late to pursue my dreams" or "I don't have time to pursue my dreams."

This belief shows feeling not good enough, lack of imagination and intuition.

"I don't need anyone."

This belief shows a feeling of disconnection, lack of clarity, of protection, and disappointment.

Exercise: Confronting Your Self-Limiting Money Beliefs

List 10 of your self-limiting money beliefs and answer the following questions (Hoobyar et al., 2013):

1. If I change this belief, who would it affect?
2. Is this belief true?
3. Is this belief empowering or limiting?

Go through each belief and complete the following sentences:

I am

_____.

People are

_____.

Life is

_____.

Part II:

Clear the Money Blocks

"Focusing your life solely on making a buck shows a poverty of ambition. It asks too little of yourself. And it will leave you unfulfilled."

-Barack Obama

Chapter 6:

Identifying and Releasing the

Money Blockage

Money blocks may just be what are keeping you broke! Besides having healthy financial habits, what you think, feel, and subconsciously believe about money has the power to create blockages between you and achieving your financial goals. Money blocks are inherently negative. They reaffirm what you can't do, the opportunities you can't have, and the financial success that is out of reach. One way of determining whether you have a money block is to reflect on your attitude toward money and accumulating wealth. Do you feel helpless, confused, frustrated, or at a disadvantage? If so, you may have a money block worth identifying and releasing.

Four Money Blocks to Release ASAP!

Money blocks can be difficult to identify since they can show up in different aspects of your life. Here are four different types of money blocks you can identify in your life and examples of how they sound like:

1. **Release Money Blocks Related to Your Limiting Beliefs**

There are some sneaky money blocks you have carried with you from childhood. You may have been influenced by your parents' limiting money beliefs or influenced by the community or upbringing you had. Money blocks related to limiting money beliefs will typically sound like a negative truth about your life. For example, you might believe:

- Poor people were conditioned to be consumers, not producers of wealth.

- This job is the best I can do.

- I have to marry into a rich family to afford that kind of lifestyle.

On the surface, these beliefs don't seem harmful, but I have seen first-hand how debilitating they can be. Someone who believes their current job is the best they can do can work in the same position for many years, without asking for a raise or seeking to grow in their career.

2. Release Money Blocks Related to Negative Self-Talk

Thinking negatively about yourself can also create money blocks; however, speaking negatively out loud can amplify them. The danger of self-talk isn't always in what you say to yourself, but in what you hear being repeated often. If you hang around people who have a scarcity mindset when it comes to wealth building, you will end up speaking like them and believing in your lack instead of your abundance. It's also equally important to avoid people who are overly critical of you. You don't want anybody speaking negatively over your job, health, or success. Instead, you want to surround yourself with people who have encouraging words to speak to you, so these words become self-fulfilling prophecies over your life. Stop, pause, and reflect when you hear yourself repeating these phrases out loud:

- I am just a dreamer.

- I can't pay off this debt.

- My boss doesn't like me.

- I hate my job.

- I am broke.

- I will die broke.

- I could never live in that neighborhood.

3. Release Money Blocks Related to Nonspecific Goals

There's nothing worse than a nonspecific goal that isn't tied to a plan or purpose. When these random goals are left for long, money blocks tend to develop around them. You will find any excuse in the book to delay working on these goals, and after years of putting them on hold, you will feel unmotivated to pursue them. The general rule of thumb is, if your financial goal matters to you, you must create a plan of action to accomplish it; otherwise, it may remain a fantasy. Give your goals a specific timeline, attach them to a deeper purpose, and make sure they are actionable. Examples of nonspecific goals include:

- I will pay off my debt.

- I have to start saving.

- One day I want to own a house.

- I need to work on my credit score.

- I need a financial adviser.

4. Release Money Blocks Related to Unresolved Emotions or Grudges You Hold Against People

Holding on to jealousy or anger against people may cause more harm to you than it does to them. When you are harboring grudges against other people, you are opening yourself to more and more negative energy (don't forget that like energy attracts like energy). This creates a ton of money blocks within you, and other undesirable energetic blocks, such as mental and emotional blocks. The best way to reverse the negative effects of holding grudges is by forgiving those that have hurt you and redirecting your energy to something positive, like focusing on your financial goals. Whenever you start feeling envious or resentful toward someone, turn the energy around by thinking about something you are truly grateful for. Here are a few examples of what holding a grudge would sound like in your mind:

- I will never trust them again.

- I am better off alone.

- Nobody understands me.

- Men/women are trash.

Three Steps for Releasing Money Blocks

Once you have identified your money blocks, you can practice the following three steps to release them:

Step 1: Acknowledge

Acknowledge your limiting money beliefs, blocks, and money stories.

Step 2: Process

Come to terms with and understand why you have held on to these limiting money beliefs and perceptions for so many years.

Step 3: Release

Once you have acknowledged and processed the blockages stored in your body, release them by choosing your own new and fresh emotions. If you had previously thought the belief was true, you will receive some form of charge, sensation, or heaviness within the body when releasing it. As you bring to mind the limiting belief, following the guidelines outlined below:

1. Surrender/Accept
2. Focus
3. Breathe
4. Shift

Exercise: Removing Money Struggles

Let us begin with deep breathing to get you in a relaxed and calm state of mind.

Sit in a comfortable position free from all distraction.

Allow yourself to take a deep breathe in . . . filling your stomach like a balloon.

And allow the breath to move up the spine.

As the breath moves up the spine, fill the stomach, chest, the throat, the face until it reaches the top of your head.

Hold at the top of the head and slowly exhale. Bringing it all the way down to the base of the spine.

Again, breathe deeply . . . as you inhale . . . fill the body up with loving energy. Hold

Exhale . . . moving all the tensions, chatters, and thoughts down to your feet.

Exhale and release worries, stress, or anxiety. You are ready to release all money woes, struggles, and anxieties—because they no longer serve you.

Imagine the sun is right in front of you. Feel the power from the fiery rays of this sun. This sun, which activates the solar plexus, will burn through all money blocks and fear you have toward money struggles or hardships. This powerful sun energy will boost your self-worth, self-respect and personal power to overcome any money adversities you are currently experiencing.

Now, as you breathe in deeply, imagine the sun moving into your body and fill your stomach center with the sun rays. Hold.

When you exhale, imagine the sun moves out of your stomach. When you inhale, let the sun move into your stomach and move out when you exhale.

Continue this breathing movement. As you breathe, let the sun in and out of your stomach.

Cup your hands together and slowly raise your hands and place them on your stomach. Continue to breathe deeply. Do not judge the sensation; just freely feel your stomach as you continue to breathe deeply.

As you continue to place your hands on your stomach, think of your money struggles. Think of a money situation you are in whether you feel stuck, scarcity, or lack of opportunities; allow yourself to feel the emotions. You now wish to be free from the money panic, denial, and anger.

Continue to focus on the situation in your mind's eye. Replay the situation from start to finish. Allow any emotions to come to the heart surface. Do not hold back, do not judge the feeling, just allow the emotions to flow.

How did you feel when you realized you were down to your last penny? Is it fear, panic, depression, anger? Whatever you are feeling, do not judge it . . . just feel the emotion.

Hold this situation in your mind's eye for a few moments.

Where do you feel the heaviest or feel tension in your body?

Focus on that area of heaviness or tension. Is there any heaviness in the stomach, in the back, neck, shoulders, head? Wherever there's tension, move the sun that's within and place your focus in that area; breathe and move the sun energy in and out of the area. This technique will help loosen any suppressed or stagnant money emotions. Continue to focus and breathe loving energy on that area.

Now, smile as you continue to focus and breathe on that area of heaviness.

Begin to send love and forgiveness to any tension or heaviness from the past. Continue to inhale and exhale the sun energy through any tension and heaviness until the tension starts to dissipate.

Now, go back and focus on that same money situation that caused you sleepless nights, that caused you the feeling of worry, shame, and depression.

Replay the situation from start to finish. Allow the emotions to come back up to the surface.

Locate and focus on that area of heaviness or tension. As you focus, continue to breathe the sun energy in and out of the area. Send love to the area of heaviness or tension until the tension starts to loosen up.

Smile as you breathe loving energy in and out of the tension.

If you feel any heaviness or tension in another part of your body, focus on that area as you breathe the sun energy. If not, you can stay where you are.

Repeat another round until you have released the blockage.

Place your focus back on your tummy. Continue to move the sun energy through your stomach center.

Expand this sun energy outside of you . . . five feet away . . . 10 feet away . . . 20 feet away. Continue to expand this energy as far as you can.

Now, it is time to come back to awareness. Place your hands down to your lap. As you slowly count back from 10, start awakening your body from the toes to eyes.

Welcome back.

How do you feel?

To access the version of this meditation visit: nandaleross.com/mind-your-money-girl-book/.

Assignment: Forgiveness List

Forgiving someone or yourself means loving yourself enough to let go of the resentment, anger, and grudges. These emotions, when prolonged, no longer serve you. It's time to release and forgive. When you practice forgiveness daily, you can revolutionize your money relationship and speed up the money manifestation.

Forgiveness will help clear up any negative energy so you can stop attracting old and tired money experiences.

Begin this exercise by recalling each of the money stories listed in the Money Story Exercises. Incorporate the forgiveness affirmation in the sample while feeling the emotions. If you have difficulties feeling, you can visualize the phrases in your mind: "I forgive," "I'm sorry," "I love," and "I'm letting go."

Sample:

I forgive_____(r ecall what happened). I'm sorry for holding on to this_____(describe the emotion you felt at the time of the event) for too long. I am sending love to this situation for healing. I release this situation to raise my money vibration. I am thankful for the lessons this situation taught me.

Complete sample:

I forgive the repo man and the lender for repossessing my vehicle. I'm sorry for holding on to this resentment for too long. I am sending love to this experience for healing. I release this situation to raise my money vibration. I give thanks for the lesson this experience taught me.

To access the PDF of this exercise visit: nandaleross.com/mind-your-money-girl-book/.

Exercise: Love and Forgiveness Visualization

This exercise is similar to the last one, "Remove Money Struggles"; however, we will focus on the heart center instead of the stomach area.

So, let's begin with deep breathing to get you in a relaxed and calm state of mind.

Sit in a comfortable position free from all distraction.

Allow yourself to take a deep breathe in . . . filling your stomach like a balloon

And allow the breath to move up the spine.

As the breath moves up the spine, fill up the stomach, chest, the throat, the face until it reaches the top of your head.

Hold at the top of the head and slowly exhale. Bring it all the way down to the base of the spine.

Repeat five times

Focus on your chest. Breathe deeply in and out of the heart center with bright light; you can use the color green, pink, or any other color that suits you.

As you breathe through your heart, fill your heart with the light of love and compassion.

Continue to focus on the heart center as you breathe in and out of your chest area.

Focusing and breathing through the heart opens the heart chakra, the center of compassion, empathy, love, and forgiveness

Clasp your hands together and slowly raise your hands and place on your chest. Continue to breathe deeply. Don't judge the sensation; just freely feel your heart as you continue to breathe deeply.

As you continue to focus on your heart center, think of the person who has hurt you or a situation that may have caused you pain. As you think of this person or situation, allow yourself to feel the emotions because you wish to be free from anger and resentment.

Continue to focus on the situation in your mind's eye. Replay the situation from start to finish. Allow any emotions to come to the heart surface. Don't hold back, don't judge the feeling, just allow the emotions to flow.

What feelings do you have toward the situation? Are they anger, shame, guilt, confusion? Whatever you're feeling, don't judge it . . . just feel the emotion.

Hold this situation in your mind's eye for a few moments.

Where do you feel the heaviest or tension on your body?

Focus on that area of heaviness or tension. As you focus, breathe loving energy in and out of the area. This technique will help loosen any tension or stagnant energy. You can use any color you like as long as you continue to focus and breathe loving energy on that area.

Smile as you continue to focus and breathe on that area of heaviness.

Now, go back and focus on that situation that caused you so much pain. Think of the person who has hurt you so bad. Think of that situation you didn't deserve to have happened to you.

Replay the situation from start to finish. Allow the emotions to come back to the surface.

Locate and focus on that area of heaviness or tension. As you focus, continue to breathe loving energy in and out of the area.

Smile as you breathe in loving energy in and out of the tension.

Repeat the steps until the heaviness dissipates.

Replay the situation from start to finish. Allow the emotions to come back up to the surface.

Locate and focus on that area of heaviness or tension. As you focus, continue to breathe loving energy in and out of the area for a few more minutes.

Smile as you breathe in loving energy to release the blockage, to release the pain and trauma.

Place your focus back on your heart center. Continue to move the love energy through your heart center.

Expand this love energy outside of you . . . five feet away . . . 10 feet away . . . 20 feet away. Continue to expand this energy as far as you can.

Now, it is time to come back to awareness. Place your hands in your lap. As you slowly count back from 10, start awakening your body from the toes to eyes.

Welcome back.

How do you feel?

To access the version of this meditation visit:
nandaleross.com/mind-your-money-girl-book/.

Chapter 7:

Rewrite Your Money Habits

Whether you are fascinated by novelties or get a thrill from spending money, your money habits and triggers can lead you toward financial independence or financial ruin. I'm sure you are screaming through your reading device, "Nan! Show me how to break my negative money habits!" The truth is you don't have to break them in order to change them; all you need to do is identify your negative money habits and replace them with habits that are aligned with your financial goals. Below is a list of common money habits that can lead to a financial crisis:

1. Emotional Spending

As discussed in Chapter 2, emotional spending is the act of making financial decisions, like purchasing an item, because of a feeling or wanting to cover up a strong emotion. Emotional spenders are more likely to make a purchase because they feel bored, undervalued, stressed, nervous, excited, or unhappy. There's nothing wrong with spoiling yourself with a trip to the nail salon or buying a gadget you had been eyeing for a few months. However, if you are spending a good portion of your money on non-essential items whenever you are looking for a distraction from processing your feelings, you run the risk of overspending or even worse - overcharging on your credit card!

How to overcome it: Give yourself a monthly budget to spend on non-essential items or experiences, like clothing, entertainment, wining and dining. Hold yourself accountable to this budget and simply decline invitations when you have maxed out your monthly allowance.

2. Compulsive Purchases

The best way to explain a compulsive purchase is the bulk buying of toilet paper we saw taking place when Covid-19 was turning from a virus to a global pandemic. Many shoppers bought a year's supply of toilet paper, thinking they wouldn't get another chance to go out and restock on goods. Compulsive purchasing is about accommodating needs that don't exist. No one needs 60 packs of toilet paper in a single month, 10 cases of soda, or 20 pairs of socks because they are special. I had to stop browsing in stores to get a grip on my compulsive shopping habit. I could spend hundreds of dollars in two hours, purchasing items that were on sale (that was my million-dollar excuse). My compulsive spending became so serious, I had to get loan   to accommodate my expensive habit.

How to overcome it: Ask yourself what use the item will serve. If you are purchasing a designer handbag or expensive heels when you already have three, ask yourself what purpose it will serve. Are your other three red bottoms worn out? Have they become too small for you? Reasons like "I don't have this color" or "My other designer handbags aren't on trend" don't count!

3. Thinking Credit Is Like Money

Be honest: How many times have you thought of credit as being free money? I remember enjoying the swiping sound of my credit card going through the card machine. I could literally swipe and forget that at the end of the month, I would need to pay the money I owe, plus a ridiculous amount of interest. Credit cards are easily misused because they give you access to cash without the burden of feeling like you are spending your own money. The truth is, it's more expensive to purchase an item with a credit card than it is to pay for it with a normal debit card, since your credit card will always charge you added interest.

How to overcome it: Live within your means. If you cannot afford something, keep a note of it and save toward it. Trust me, there's nothing more gratifying now than being able to collect an item I have been saving up for. I know that I can enjoy my item without having to calculate how much I owe the bank for it.

4. Excessive Monthly Subscriptions

Many years ago, monthly subscriptions used to be for premium magazines, videos, and catalogues. Nowadays, you can get a monthly subscription for pretty much anything. There are companies that offer monthly subscriptions for beauty products, fitness, TV on demand, video streaming, and hobby-based crafts. Individually, they may not break your bank, but when you add them all up, you realize they can come to the price of one month's utility bills or even savings.

How to overcome it: Have you ever stopped and asked yourself if you really need *that* much entertainment. Do you use your mobile app subscription? Or are you flipping through Netflix, Amazon Prime, and Hulu streaming devices or cable TV on a daily basis? If the answer is no, you can find ways to reduce your subscriptions to only those you actually need, like your Wi-Fi or cable subscription.

5. Shopping Peer Pressure

Oh boy, I think it's story time again! If there's anyone who knows about shopping peer pressure, it's me. Growing up, I always had a sense of wanting to prove myself to others, but this need for validation became increasingly present in my life when I was making enough money to buy all of the items people envied. I thought to myself, "Ha! Finally I can live that luxury lifestyle that all of my peers desire." I became that girl with clothes in her closet that still had tags on them because they hadn't been worn. My focus was never to wear most of my clothes but to have the bragging rights of saying, "Yes, I own that!" I felt pressured to live an expensive lifestyle I could barely keep up with, and my desire for validation became a compulsion I couldn't control.

How to overcome it: Overcoming the pressure to spend money and prove I could afford the "soft life" wasn't easy. However, fighting my negative self-talk and reminding myself that my value didn't lie in the things that I owned, but the person who I was, helped me gradually let go of the need to prove a point with how I spent my money.

6. Being a Workaholic

We were led to believe that if we want to make our dreams come true, we must hustle, sacrifice, and suffer in the process. This is far from the truth. In my experience, working 14 to 16 hours a day placed an untold amount of stress on me that clouded my financial judgment, led to insomnia, cost me two marriages, and jeopardized the relationship I had with my son. If you believe it takes hard work to be successful, then don't be surprised if you need to sacrifice your well-being to become successful. Work that you don't enjoy or that you aren't passionate about will always be hard. Although, if you are passionate about your work, it won't seem like hard work (and you won't have to sacrifice aspects of your life for you to succeed in it).

How to overcome it: Stop picking jobs for the paycheck, and let your passion lead you to projects and business you are inspired to make work. If you can't quit your day job just yet, make your passion project a side-hustle that you work on during weekends. Who knows? In a few years you may be making more money from your side-hustle than your day job.

Chapter 8:

Spending Money Consciously

Have you ever been the kind of person who spends money without thinking about where it's going and consequently end up broke before the month is over? I'd like to think that many people have been through this phase, at least once in their lives, and have come out on the other side carrying a lot of debt they couldn't afford.

One of the ways to break unhealthy money habits is to become a conscious spender. In simple language, a conscious spender is someone who considers every purchase they make and spends on things that will bring added value to their lives. Of course, what one person perceives as valuable will be different from the next person; in both cases, however, only items seen as providing value are purchased.

Conscious spenders also prioritize what matters most. They are willing to make trade-offs to ensure their family's basic needs are met and that all monthly bills have been paid. In other words, these spenders have mastered the art of delayed gratification. A conscious spender will put off eating out at a fancy restaurant so that they can restock their refrigerator with groceries. Before taking a vacation, a conscious spender will make sure their mortgage is up-to-date or that their children's tuition is paid.

I'm sure you're starting to see the main difference between a conscious spender and an emotional spender. Both spenders have money, although they put their money to work differently. A conscious spender spends money in exchange for value while an emotional spender spends money in exchange for feeling good. The only problem with spending money to feel good is that the "feeling" only lasts a few minutes or a couple of hours, yet value can last a lifetime.

What is your big reason for spending money on the products or activities you like? Are you seeking valuable products or activities that will improve your well-being or lifestyle, or are you just trying to numb the pain of ordinary life or find distractions so you don't have to address your current life situation? If becoming a conscious spender sounds interesting to you, then you need to commit to making purchases that carry the biggest impact in your life. Focus on buying things that make you happier, smarter, healthier, and more confident. If you spend your money in this way, you will never feel guilty for spending your money.

Don't Be a Hoarder

Popular TV shows taking us into the lives of extreme hoarders have shown us the extent of chaos hoarding can bring into our lives. I remember watching an episode with my mom one time and seeing a mother who had lost her job and didn't have a good relationship with her children because of her extreme hoarding. All she had was her stuff. The sad part is that some of what she owned was valuable and probably would've sold for a fortune, but all of her valuable goods looked worthless among a pile of other things.

Everybody has that sentimental piece of jewelry or garment they don't use anymore, but prefer to keep because of the value it holds. However, if everything we own is considered "sentimental" and everything we buy (on top of what we own) is considered sentimental too, then we have a problem on our hands.

Hoarding usually begins as a way to compensate for a feeling or experience we had in the past, where we felt out of control. For example, a person who grew up in a home where food was always scarce and some nights they would sleep on an empty stomach may develop a habit of hoarding food as an adult. They may become a coupon queen or king and chase after the next bulk deal they could find (there's a show on TV about this too).

Sometimes hoarding can be associated with a self-limiting belief. For example, a woman who grew up thinking "Only beautiful women get respect" may develop a habit of purchasing the latest beauty treatments, fashion trends, hair extensions, makeup products, and anything else they can get their hands on, so they can achieve the kind of beauty standard they believe will earn them respect.

Hoarding never feels good, even to a hoarder. This is because the void they feel inside cannot be satisfied with the hundreds of things they own. It's one of those voids that needs to be acknowledged, processed, and released (check out Chapter 7) so that the attachment to the things you own can disappear.

If you desire to go from hoarder to conscious spender, take a moment to ask yourself the following questions whenever you are about to make a purchase:

- Do I love this item? (Liking it isn't good enough.)

- Do I love how this item makes me feel? (Does the item elevate your mood?)

- Do I need this item as part of my lifestyle? (Notice I wrote "need" and not "want")

- Do I have space for this item in my home, car, office, backyard, and so forth?

- Do I have a plan to start using it immediately? (Oh, you do? What's your plan?)

- Can I get this item somewhere else, for an affordable price? (Conscious spenders are smart shoppers too)

- Does holding on to this item keep me in the past?

- Will owning this item help me achieve my personal goals?

Don't Be Cheap, Either!

While hoarders purchase items they don't need, cheapskates would rather compromise on their basic needs to save a dollar. The two are polar opposites. Now, I don't want you to confuse being cheap with being frugal. Frugal people are penny pinchers; however, they understand that there are some things that don't come cheap. Unlike cheapskates, frugal people don't mind paying a premium if it comes with added value. A cheapskate believes the only way to own anything in life is to pay the lowest amount of money possible. Many times, this means compromising on the quality of products. A cheapskate doesn't mind shopping for expired food products just so they can save a few dollars on their grocery bill.

Cheapskates believe they are better at handling money than other spenders because they hardly spend any of it. I would beg to differ. Since cheapskates compromise on value and quality, they are more likely to replace products after a few months due to faults or poor design. Imagine a cheap person and a frugal person walking into an appliance store, looking to purchase a brand new coffeemaker. The cheap person is reluctant to enter the store because he thinks he can get a quality second-hand coffeemaker from a local thrift store. The frugal person is happy to enter the store because they haven't been able to have their morning cup of coffee ever since their previous one broke.

A shop attendant takes both spenders to the coffeemaker aisle. "Don't you have any demos on sale?" asks the cheapskate. The shop attendant says unfortunately they don't sell their demos to paying customers. Instead of looking at the different models and the features of each coffeemaker, the cheapskate compares the prices. Ideally, he wants to pay the lowest price so he can feel like a winner. Eventually, he finds the lowest priced coffeemaker with minimal features and no warranty, and heads to the pay point.

The frugal person takes his time comparing the various coffeemakers and looks for one that is excellent quality, but at a reasonable price point. He selects a few of his favorites and does a quick Internet search to assess its reviews from other customers. After reading a few reviews, he ends up choosing the one that is most reliable and uses the least amount of power. About a year after both spenders bought their coffeemakers, the cheapskate had replaced his machine three times, but the frugal person is still holding on to the one he purchased.

Tips to Make Conscious Spending a Lifestyle

You are in control of your money. The belief that you're not is what makes you handle your money mindlessly. You have the final say on whether you will buy a Starbucks coffee every morning before work. Conscious spending is all about regaining control of your finances and saying no to temptation or reckless spending. Here are a few tips to make conscious spending a lifestyle:

1. Keep Track of Your Spending

Tell yourself that no dollar will leave your purse or your bank account without your knowing where it's going. Even if you have change left over from a transaction, count those coins and track how you spend them. You may want to activate your bank notifications to show up on your phone, if you don't already have them activated. Trust me, I know how difficult it is having to see your bank balance drop, but perhaps it's the wakeup call you need.

2. Open Your Bills

I used to be afraid to check my mailbox or open my bank account in fear of past due invoices or negative balances. I wouldn't wear the color red since I had a subconscious fear of letters in red; I took the color red as meaning warning, error, danger, or going under. My fear of opening my bills became a money block because it meant I was perpetuating the cycle of debt in my life. I had to learn the hard way that confronting my debt was the only way I could work through it and overcome it.

3. Watch Your Credit Score

Your credit score can open so many financial doors for you—or close them shut. It's in your best interest to keep watch of your credit score and work on improving it. One of the ways to improve your score is to pay your creditors on time and avoid negative balances. Another way to improve your credit score, which is less spoken about, is taking on more credit. This may sound like irresponsible advice, but hear me out. If you are maintaining your current debt and making enough money to pay your creditors consistently, taking out more credit can help you improve your credit score. You don't have to max out your new credit; simply buy something small and pay it off at the end of the month. Do this consistently and watch your credit score skyrocket!

4. Trust Your Intuition

If something feels too expensive, it probably is! Price is highly subjective because every shopper has a different budget. If you know your current budget and the item far exceeds it, you can safely say, "This is worth saving up for." There's no shame in saving up for an item or having to pay it off in small chunks before you can own it. The truth of the matter is there's someone out there who needs to save up for the kind of lifestyle you can afford so effortlessly, and there's also someone out there who lives a lifestyle you have posted on your vision board.

Exercise: Get Your Money Together

In the early 2000s, I found myself blaming others for my financial problems. I blamed my ex-husband for walking out on me. I blamed my family for talking me into getting married at 19. I blamed the religious organization for ingraining the belief that striving for success is a bad thing. I blamed friends who took advantage of my money, time, and energy. I was blaming everyone for my problems because I was too afraid to own up to my sh*t. I was so fearful of money that I ignored looking at my bank account. You know, the feeling of anxiety of seeing your money in red? I dreaded opening my utility bills and credit card statements, making sure I paid only the "amount due" or the minimum payment.

I didn't even know how many automatic withdrawals from memberships and subscriptions were eating up my money. I was unaware of when all my bills were due. I was hoping I had enough money in the bank to cover the charges and insufficient fund fees. I was miserable because I couldn't admit I might have done something wrong. It wasn't until I began listening to my gut feeling to be accountable for my financial behaviors. It was time to face my financial struggles and do something about them.

Do you think the relationship would last if you neglected your partner, husband, family, and friends? I don't think so, baby girl! When you ignore your finances, showing no love to your money, you are compromising the most important relationship you will ever have: Your money. So, I decided to stop chasing my ex-husband for child support and take ownership of my finances.

The good news is that you are taking the necessary steps to heal your wounds to rebuild the relationship with your moolah. In the next exercise, you will take the time to open each one of your credit card statements, utility bills, and bank accounts to access the amount you owe, due date, and remaining balance. Don't worry about how you will cover the expense, even if there's a shortage.

Turn to Appendix A and complete the monthly budget worksheet. The exercise is designed to help you re-evaluate your finances. After completing your monthly budget, take a look at some of the places your money is going. At this point, all I want you to do is simply observe and reflect.

To access the PDF version of this worksheet visit: nandaleross.com/mind-your-money-girl-book/.

Part III:

Reprogram the Mindset to Create a

New Money Reality

"Be thankful for what you have; you'll end up having more. If you concentrate on what you don't have, you will never ever have enough."

-Oprah Winfrey

Chapter 9:

Secure the Bag

If you have a social media presence, you'll be familiar with the term "secure the bag." Securing the bag is about making the necessary lifestyle changes so you can go after the goals you desire to achieve, and make a lot of money in the process. No one can secure the bag staying within their comfort zone. Look, if your method of making money worked, you'd probably be financially set by now. Clearly your methods aren't working and to see positive results, you will need to get uncomfortable and do things differently.

I speak to my clients a lot about securing the bag, and let me tell you something, all of them know exactly what they want and how they want it. However, when it comes to taking action on these goals, many of them feel either unprepared or under-resourced in taking the first steps.

I often remind them that the first few steps don't require much preparation or resources; all they require is a determination to get on with it! The brand Nike summarized it best in their slogan, "Just do it." Securing the bag is about just doing it and letting the journey help you figure out what you need and the best next step. No one is ever 100% confident when they start anything. Even those who have plans don't have the entire plan figured out. Delaying your progress because you feel unprepared or under-resourced is an excuse we won't accept in this moment and moving forward. Before we move on, here are four ways you can start securing your bag right now:

1. Read a New Book Every Month

Knowledge is power because you don't know what you don't know. There are so many opportunities around you that you cannot see or access because you can't identify them. Your knowledge capacity simply isn't large enough to recognize some of the opportunities that may exist in your environment. So how do you fix this? You read a new book every month, on different topics. Make sure that each book exposes you to a new skill, mindset, principle, or habit. As you expand your mind, you will realize that you are more powerful than you think you are and there are so many money-making opportunities around you.

2. Change Your Circle

Getting value from what you buy is good; securing the bag, however, is about getting value from every area of your life, including your friendship circles. When last have you done a friendship audit and assessed the amount of value you are gaining from your friendships? If you are the smartest, happiest, and most driven person in your circle, you aren't gaining any value from those around you. Ideally, you want to be around people who are smarter than you and more successful so that you can learn from them and become more valuable.

3. If it Doesn't Scare You, Aim Higher

Securing the bag is about doing what everyone is too afraid to do so you can live how everyone dreams of living. If you are determined to pursue your goals, get ready to step out of your comfort zone, hang around new people, attend new types of events around town, and expose yourself to new knowledge. All of this newness will feel overwhelming at first, but trust me, very soon it will become your new normal. If your goals are worth pursuing they are supposed to scare you or stretch you so much that you become unrecognizable to your old self. If your goals aren't scaring you, you're probably still in your comfort zone. Dream a little bigger, aim a little higher, and allow yourself to grow into the person fit for the life you desire.

Securing Your Savings

Part of securing the bag involves securing your savings. There's no way to get around it; you simply need to spend less and save more to accumulate wealth. Having money saved also helps you have the advantage in situations. For instance, if you know that you have to complete a course to qualify as a teacher in a specific discipline, you can easily pay for the course with your savings, without stressing about where the money will come from. If your child is heading off to college, your savings account will help you pay for the tuition without having to take out a student loan.

People often use the words "savings" and "investments" interchangeably, but they refer to two different concepts. Savings and investments are both financial vehicles for accumulating wealth, although they play different roles in your life. When you save money, you stash it away in an interest-bearing savings account and allow it to stay there until the day you need to use it for emergencies or specific financial goals, like starting a business. Investing money on the other hand refers to expending money to achieve a profit into shares, property, or commercial ventures. This could be a 401(k), stocks, foreign currency, securities, real estate, or a business. I'm a true believer in multiple streams of income.

You don't need to invest in the stock market to save money and secure the bag. Simple budget cuts, done consistently, can have a huge impact on your savings. For example, if you found a way to cut back on $100 each month (by reducing your spending on various goods), you would have $1,200 cash in 12 months. Instead of spending the money on meaningless things, you could stash it away in an interest-bearing savings account (this is how you make your money work for you). If every year you increased your monthly savings by $50 (saving $150 in year two, $200 in year three,

$250 in year four, etc), in five years you would have $12,000 in savings, excluding the compounding interest you would have earned on your money. This would be enough money to put as a down payment on a home, buy a car, start a business, or pay off some or all of your debt.

When it comes to how much you should be saving every month, the answer is completely dependent on how much income you earn on a monthly basis and how much of that income goes toward settling debt. The amount of money you end up saving will also depend on your age, needs, and lifestyle preferences. If you hardly go out on weekends and don't really have bad spending habits, you may be able to save more on a monthly basis than someone who loves going out and enjoying the finer things in life. We can't forget the elephant in the room: Debt. Debt can interfere with your savings plan, especially when it takes up a huge chunk of your income. The best solution in that case is to focus on paying off any high-interest debt (any debt that charges you 15% or higher in interest) before you can begin saving money.

Two Simple Budget Ratios to Help You on Your Savings Journey

Living on a budget can reduce a lot of stress related to your finances. Your budget tells you how much you have allocated to certain needs or wants, and sets limits that you cannot cross. These limits aren't a form of punishment; rather, they help you reach your financial goals without feeling like you have made too many compromises. Think of a budget as being a healthy spending routine to kickstart your savings journey. By following this routine, you will save more money than you ever have before.

When it comes to creating a budget, there are several methods and techniques you can use, like focusing on paying off your debt first, cutting up your credit cards and paying with cash only, or going cold turkey and cutting out a few expenses. These methods and techniques have worked for many people before; however, I have found using ratios to be beneficial for two reasons. First, ratios don't cut out any expenses, so it's great for beginners who aren't used to sticking to a budget and don't like the sound of going cold turkey. Second, ratios can be adjusted over time and less money can be allocated to certain ratio categories, which makes this budgeting method rather flexible.

There are two budget ratios I propose to my clients. The only difference between these ratios is the amount of money allocated to different categories.

75/15/10

The 75/15/10 budget ratio splits your monthly income in three ways: 75% goes toward monthly expenses, 15% goes toward your savings, and 10% goes toward investments or repaying debt (D, 2021). You can follow this budget ratio by following these easy steps:

Step 1: Calculate Your Monthly Income

In general, your total monthly income should come from your salary, however, if you have other sources of income, you should add them up and reach a value encompassing all sources of income you receive on a monthly basis.

Step 2: Allocate 75% for Living Expenses

Your living expenses will include items like your rent or mortgage payments, health insurance, car insurance, groceries, utility bills, gas for your car, childcare, and so forth. Dedicate 75% of your income to your living expenses. If your expenses far exceed your monthly income, you would need to have a look at where your money is going and make some necessary cost reductions.

Step 3: Allocate 15% for Savings

This category is very broad and to make your life easier, you can break it down into three categories. First, you need to save toward your retirement. This is regardless of how old you are (in fact, the younger you start, the better). You also need to dedicate a portion of your savings to your emergency fund. An emergency fund is a savings account you create for rainy days or to cover you in unforeseen events, like hospitalization or losing your job.

Ideally, you should have a minimum of three to six months' worth of income in your emergency fund to protect yourself in unlikely situations. Lastly, you will also need to dedicate a portion of your savings to your personal goals. Are you looking to go on holiday soon? Do you want to remodel your home? All of these goals will need cash, so start saving toward them.

Step 4: Allocate 10% for Investments or Debt

When debt piles up, it can feel like a never-ending cycle. Fortunately, by setting aside money to repay your debt every month, you can gradually work toward eliminating it for good. Paying off your debt on a monthly basis may also improve your credit score, which over time, qualifies you for big-ticket loan purchases (such as buying a car or a house on a loan). If you cover your debt as part of the 75% allocated to living expenses, you can use the remaining 10% to invest in stocks and other types of assets or securities.

50/30/20

The 50/30/20 budget ratio breaks down your monthly income into three categories: needs, wants, and financial goals (Vansomeren, 2011). This ratio helps savers become aware of their financial habits and limit overspending while also limiting under-saving. Below is a step-by-step guideline to using the 50/30/20 budget ratio:

Step 1: Calculate Your Monthly Income

Similar to the previous ratio, you need to begin by calculating your monthly income. If you receive income from sources other than your primary job, add these incomes together and come up with one all-encompassing value.

Step 2: Create Your Allocations

The next step is to create a spending threshold for each category. In other words, you would need to multiply your total monthly income by 0.50 for your needs, 0.30 for your wants, and 0.20 for your financial goals. Your needs may include items like groceries, transport, mortgage, and utilities (things you cannot go a month without paying for). Your wants may include items like dining out, monthly subscriptions, buying new clothes, or participating in hobbies. Lastly, your financial goals may include items like paying off your debt, saving toward retirement, or starting a business venture.

Step 3: Plan Your Budget Around Your Allocations

If your take-home salary is $2,000, you would allocate $1,000 ($2,000 x 0.50) to your needs, $600 ($2,000 x 0.30) to your wants, and $400 ($2,000 x 0.20) to your financial goals. It's important to maintain these allocations and try to not overspend on any particular category. If your priority is to focus on your financial goals, you can take a portion of your wants budget and add it to your financial goals budget. This would mean spending less on wants on that particular month (this is a sacrifice you need to be willing to make).

Chapter 10:

Prepare for a Money Mindset

Makeover

Do you deserve to have money? Are you good enough to accumulate wealth?

You may be quick to say yes, but do you honestly believe you deserve a life of abundance?

The belief that money is hard to make comes from a scarcity mindset. A scarcity mindset seeks lack as being the norm and abundance as being rare or a matter of luck. Many people who play the lottery do so because they want to "get lucky." Those who drop a coin in a money pond do so because they hope one day they may "get lucky" and live the life of their dreams. There's no such thing as luck for someone who believes they deserve to be wealthy, even if it means not working as hard as some of their peers.

The scarcity mindset will always add a touch of suffering to everything you do. Everything is a struggle. Creating a business proposal is a struggle. Applying for jobs is a struggle. Putting on a cute outfit and attending networking events is a struggle. How do you honestly think you will achieve some of the extraordinary goals you have if even the smallest tasks toward your goal feel like a struggle?

Those with a scarcity mentality don't truly believe they deserve the kind of lifestyle they envision. I mean yes, they think it looks beautiful, and every day they look at pictures of their dream lifestyle on their phone or on their vision board, but deep down they are disconnected from their desire.

How come?

It's simple: They don't believe they are valuable enough to have what they desire.

A common belief goes like this:

How could a person like me live a life like that?

People with a scarcity mindset aren't short of ideas or talent, but they lack faith in themselves to turn these ideas into tangible products or services worth something.

To attract wealth and wealth-building opportunities, you would need to adopt the opposite of a scarcity mindset, which is the abundance mindset. Many people think you must be rich to think abundantly, but this isn't true. Think about all of the successful entrepreneurs who have gone on to accumulate wealth. When they were starting out, all they had was their million-dollar idea and an unshakable desire to succeed. Did they face challenges and failures? Of course they did! But something else kept them in the game: Their abundance mindset. They knew that the world needed their ideas and talents, and so they wouldn't give up until these ideas became influential. They shared their value to anyone who would listen and eventually, what started off as an idea became a movement, business, or cutting-edge innovation.

If like energy attracts like energy, you need to think abundantly and live abundantly to attract abundance. Listen to the way you speak about yourself or about your capabilities. Look at what you are currently spending your money on and assess whether it is attracting abundance or scarcity. Look at your associations and assess whether they are influencing you toward abundance or scarcity. Time is moving, and whether you are aware of it or not, you are constantly moving toward an abundant life or a life of scarcity.

Exercise: What Do You Like About Yourself?

For this exercise, I would like you to think about what you like about yourself. Think about something you feel to be true. Is it the way you make people laugh? Is it that you're a healer? Or, is it that you help others find employment? Add some form of representation about this quality. What picture do you see yourself doing? How do you feel while you're performing this task? What are you saying to the other person?

Understand and write these activities down on a piece of paper.

Do you see yourself performing this task in a still picture, or in a movie? Is it in color or black and white? Is it bright or dull? Is it full size or miniature size? Make a note of these characteristics too. Do you see yourself performing the task or are you outside of it? What do you hear yourself saying?

Relive the experience and become associated with it to strengthen the experience. Make the vision bigger and brighter.

The next step is to think about what you like about yourself in the future. Think about what you want to add or enhance about who you are? Have you noticed anything different? Maybe a new place? New types of people? Did you enhance your skills? If you saw yourself making people laugh in the first part of the vision, do you see yourself making a crowd or audience laugh in the future? Record or write down your photograph or movie of yourself in the future. Over the next few days, practice this exercise again and connect to the power of who you are now and who you desire to be in the future.

Make Up Your Mind: What Do You Want?

You would be shocked to find out how many people cannot articulate what it is they actually want. They might be able to point to someone else's life and say, "I want that!" but upon asking them to elaborate on what "that" is, they are speechless. Here's the thing: Our eyes can easily notice something beautiful or something worth pursuing; however, our hearts are aligned to our personal desires. We can look at the lives of the rich and famous and say, "I want that!" but ultimately, our hearts are connected to what we truly value and what we genuinely desire.

The issue is many people aren't connecting to their heart's desires. I have found that people are constantly distracted or blinded by two things: Either they are distracted by what they see others doing, or they are distracted by their unresolved emotions and negative beliefs. In other words, letting go of comparisons and competing with other people and resolving all of the inner turmoil can help people connect to their hearts and make decisions about their future that are aligned with their purpose.

I have read many books speaking about the benefit of goal setting, and sure, I agree with them. However, how effective has goal setting been in your life? Were you able to accomplish your New Year's resolutions? Have you been able to scratch off some goals you had set for the first six months or last six months of the year?

It turns out setting goals is a lot easier than accomplishing them. Along my spiritual journey, I have found another method of holding myself accountable to my desires that is far more deep-rooted than goal setting. This method is known as setting intentions. Intentions not only focus on helping you focus on a particular goal, but they also connect you to your heart's desire. Imagine how it would feel to accomplish a goal you feel deeply connected to. You wouldn't need reminders to get started or to follow through with it because accomplishing the goal is a part of your greater purpose.

When life happens and projects don't go according to plan, it's a lot easier to drop a goal than it is to drop an intention. This is because intentions are aligned to who you are, and therefore regardless of what comes and what goes, you will always find a way to overcome obstacles ahead of you and pursue what you deeply desire. You don't even need to feel motivated to carry out your intentions. Just as effortlessly as you wake up and brush your teeth in the morning, when your intentions are ingrained in you, you subconsciously act in ways that promote and empower them.

Setting Intentions: Why Do You Want It?

If you have ever found it difficult to maintain a positive outlook on your financial situation or on your financial goals, setting intentions may help you get back on track. This is because intentions dig deep to find the why behind every goal you set. It's not enough to describe what you want and set S.M.A.R.T goals that help you set parameters to your goals; you need to be aligned to the goal on a deeper level. Each goal you pursue needs to be able to answer the questions of:

1. Who am I?

2. What do I desire?

3. Why do I desire it?

If your financial goal is to be debt-free, besides setting parameters to pay off your debt, your goal must be aligned to the above questions. For example, you may write the following:

1. Who am I?

I am a child of God and I enjoy the freedom and abundance that is rightfully mine.

2. What do I desire?

I desire financial freedom so I can live a life that is authentic to who I am and resembles what I deserve.

3. Why do I desire it?

It's not a part of my life's purpose to live on the bare minimum.

Imagine for a second that every morning or every evening before you went to bed, you reflected on these three questions and answers. Don't you imagine you would feel a greater sense of purpose to become debt-free? Don't you imagine you would be inspired to relook at your finances and make decisions based on the abundance you see within yourself? This, my friend, is the power of setting intentions. By tapping into the big why you are able to dig deep and align your goals with who you are and your heart's desires.

If you are excited about setting your own intentions, I will provide you with three simple principles to remember:

1. **Your intentions must always be in the form of positive affirmations, for example:**

Financial freedom is my rightful inheritance.

2. **Your intentions must be created on the back of your current goal, for example:**

I have all the wisdom to live debt-free.

3. Your intentions must be part of a small ritual you can do regularly, for example:

I am open to receiving direction from the Universe/God on how to resolve my financial situation (the small ritual here would be having a daily moment of prayer or meditation to listen for spiritual guidance on your money matters).

Exercise: The Perfect Life

I remember in elementary school, my teachers would scold me for staring outside the window instead of paying attention to what was on the blackboard. As an adult, we lost touch with visualizing or daydreaming. Visualization is a powerful manifesting skill that we have lost. And now, it's time to regain that skillset.

This exercise will help you create a personalized mental movie of your perfect life in five areas:

1. Your career/finance or business

2. Personal development or values

3. Physical health

4. Relationships

5. Contribution to society

Every morning for the next five days, while still in the bed, visualize your perfect life. Start imaging as if you were living in that moment. Include sensory perception and strong, positive emotions, and brighten the vision and make it bigger. Don't worry about how it will happen, but visualize and believe it's true.

Day 1: Visualize your financial abundance. What are you doing to make a living? How much money is in your bank account? Where are you living? Would you have a cushion saved in the bank? Would you buy another car? Would you get out of debt? Would you buy a house?

Day 2: Visualize the personality traits or characteristics your wish to have. Is it confidence, patience, courage, motivation, optimism, willpower, drive, patience, and the like? Visualize how you would walk, talk, stand and interact with others when you have those personality characteristics.

Day 3: Visualize your ideal health. How would you maintain it? What are you doing to achieve it?

Day 4: Visualize your ideal relationships. Who are you spending time with? What are you doing with them?

Day 5: How will you contribute to society? Are you volunteering? Donating? Helping the sick or homeless? Are you a philanthropist?

For each day be sure to include the following:

1. Be in the first person. Visualize everything through your eyes.

2. Have clear and specific intentions.

3. Include details when visualizing the features.

4. Know exactly how you feel. Do you feel safe, secure, confident? For example, a house in a gated community/subdivision can make you feel safe and secure. Or, you feel good seeing your loved one's excitement as they pack their bags to go on a family cruise? Or, you feel so relaxed knowing you can pay your bills on time? The essence helps build the emotions from the features.

5. Create emotions using sensory perceptions. What do you smell, taste, touch, and hear? How's the weather, what's the aroma, what's in the background?

6. Hold the mental movie for at least one minute and replay for at least 10 minutes. The longer you keep rehashing the mental movie, the faster it will manifest.

7. Have patience.

We cannot give a deadline on the manifestation's time-frame. Allow the energy of your thoughts, emotions, and ideas to manifest your desires in the physical realm. Certain events, people, and circumstances must take place first before you can get what you desire. Therefore, you must be patient. If you have been in the state of mind of lack, mainly the lack of money for years, the manifestation may take a little longer unless you clear the unprocessed emotions. The mindset of scarcity is negative energy. Could there be limited belief, maybe from the past, this could cause you to feel lack?

We will learn how to instill confidence, self-love and forgiveness in the upcoming lessons.

Start paying attention to how your day goes and the shift in energy. Pay attention to certain people and opportunities presented to you. They will be in alignment with your clear and precise intentions. We cannot continue to call this coincidence.

Show gratitude. Being in the state of mind of gratitude is living in high vibratory frequency. The higher the frequency, the faster it is transformed in physical form. Whether you are having a good or bad day, always show gratitude. It will do a 180-degree change in circumstances, feelings, and thoughts. Trust me, I had experienced miracles when I gave appreciation to an unfavorable situation. Whenever you experience small synchronicity events (showing proof that you are on the right track), try your hardest to be thankful.

Practice these steps for at least 21 days. These new thoughts or intentions will stick in your subconscious mind. After 21 days, you will start to form a habit.

Chapter 11:

Beautify Your Money

Do you know what people are really buying when they spend $1,000 on beauty products or hair extensions? They are buying confidence! Don't get me wrong, there's nothing wrong with having the desire to own these things; however, it doesn't hurt to understand the triggers behind these purchases. The only way a big-ticket item can add any value to your life is if it answers an unmet need. Beauty enhancements answer a need, which is to provide the customer with more confidence.

Gaining confidence (without having to buy it) isn't as easy as you may think. The truth is you are not born confident, and if you're like most people, confidence doesn't come naturally. True confidence is coming to complete acceptance of yourself and identifying your strengths so you can leverage them to succeed in life. True confidence is what gives you the assurance that one day you will be a millionaire, even if your current paycheck or bank overdraft doesn't show it.

A lack of confidence not only brings about a low self-esteem, but it can also affect your earning potential.

Think about it this way: Will a person lacking in confidence schedule a meeting to ask their boss for a raise? It's highly unlikely. Even if they deserve the raise, their lack of confidence may cause them to fear having their request rejected. Now imagine a confident person being tasked with the same thing. Not only would they schedule the meeting, they would put together a 20-page document highlighting all of the projects and assignments they have been working on in the past year that qualify them for the raise.

When you believe in yourself and understand what you deserve out of life, you start to move differently. No longer are you waiting for handouts or for untrustworthy people to keep their promises. Instead, you focus on making the first move, sending that email, enrolling in that course, sending in your job application, securing that business loan, networking with those established people, and so on. Your confidence allows you to boldly walk into boardrooms or function venues you had never imagined you would walk in before, and own the room as though you were the host or hostess!

When you are truly confident, you don't have to buy confidence. It radiates from within you and it's felt by everyone you come across. When you believe in yourself, you realize just how much progress you make in a year, and this allows you to go after your financial dreams.

If your confidence has been damaged by your financial struggles, the best way to turn things around would be to commit to taking steps to better your financial situation. Committing to making changes to how you handle and spend money is such a huge step. It shows you are taking accountability for your crisis and mature enough to press the reset button and start over on a positive note.

Another way to increase your confidence is to get educated. I cannot stress enough how valuable getting educated is. An education opens economic opportunities and it is also one of the best ways to reduce the wage gap between races and genders. What's great is that no one can take your education away from you. Even if the corporate environment isn't your scene, you can start businesses or become an investor with the education you have acquired.

Believing yourself isn't an option on your wealth building journey; it's a necessity! Your confidence will help you stay motivated during rough patches and find ways to continuously challenge yourself. Here are a few money mantras you can repeat out loud, in the morning before you get out of bed or in the evening before you go to sleep:

- I am able to achieve greatness.

- I am gifted.

- I have so much value to offer the world.

- I will not stand in my own way.

- I am manifesting my heart's desires.

- My financial situation is improving.

- I am becoming financially wiser every day.

Exercise: Swish Confidence

The Swish Pattern is a neuro-linguistic programming (NLP) technique that helps you quickly deal and weaken negative thoughts. You will no longer fight with the negative thoughts but instead you will train your brain a new way of responding to the negative thoughts or triggers.

Make a list of anything in the near future where you don't feel confidence in. The more you have on the list, the better. This could be going on a job interview, asking for a raise, starting a new business or side-hustle. Identify the feeling you want to eliminate. Identify the thoughts and images that provoke low confidence or self-esteem. This will be your first representation for this exercise.

Once you have completed the list, now I want you to list a time in the past where you felt confident. It can be cooking a meal, completing a task successfully, making a financial decision. Spend some time creating a powerful and confident image. Identify the emotion you want to start feeling such as confidence or high self-esteem. Write down your second replacement image in as much detail as you can to help you solidify your visualization. This will be the second representation used in this exercise.

Take one from the list and close your eyes. Think of the trigger image (the low confidence), then start inserting the replacement image in between the trigger image. In between worrying, start imagining yourself feeling more confident

Allow the replacement image to become bigger and more vivid so that the trigger image begins a gradual disappearance.

Break the state and open your eyes.

Start from step 1 and this time, try to insert the replacement faster.

Repeat the process about five to seven times.

Test it to see what happens when you try to recall the negative trigger image, you will discover that it becomes more difficult to bring back the negative feelings.

Reflect on the results of the Swish technique in your journal.

Self-Love and Forgiveness

We have spoken about the importance of forgiving others as a way to release money blocks; however, forgiving yourself for all of the ways you misused money, fell into money scams, trusted people with your money, or weren't able to provide for yourself or your family is just as important. Think about the times you have let yourself down, like not having enough money to pay for groceries or having the comfort of your family compromised because of your poor financial decisions.

You may be able to suppress these memories, but you don't properly deal with them and forgive yourself for your past mistakes, you will always feel a sense of guilt or shame when you think about money. As you prepare to move forward on your money journey, you must be able to remove all of your money baggage and all of the "should haves" and "could haves" and step into this new phase of your life without regrets.

You are not the first person to have made money mistakes. Many of us make financial decisions without weighing the consequences first. The good news is that you are willing to own your mistakes and let go of being overly critical about your past spending habits or past money story. Below are three ways you can begin healing your financial regrets and making peace with your past:

1. Own Up to It

What are you regretful for? Come clean about the financial decisions you have made in the past that have caused you a lot of grief. Speaking your truth is liberating, and it will expose what has been eating you up inside for so many years. Write down what you are regretful for and then find someone close who you can express your regrets to. Their job isn't to counsel you but simply to listen and reassure you that you aren't alone. Some of your regrets may be:

I regret buying a house I couldn't afford.

I regret spending my children's college tuition on a shopping spree.

I regret not being able to support my family financially.

I regret accumulating so much debt.

2. Name the Belief You Were Informed By

Your financial regrets stem from beliefs that you may have felt to be true at the time. This is why your actions didn't seem out of the ordinary, dangerous, or even selfish. You believed you were doing the right thing and as such, took the actions that you did. For each regret, think about the underlying belief you were informed by and spend some time reflecting on these beliefs, considering how misinformed you were. Some of the beliefs you may write include:

I bought the house because I thought I would be the laughingstock in my circle of friends, since everybody else was a homeowner.

I spent child support on getting my hair done because I thought I deserved a reward for working so hard. I put my needs before anyone else's.

I wasn't able to support my family financially because I thought I was too good to work at a low-paying job. I undermined opportunities of work because they didn't fit my criteria.

I accumulated a lot of debt because I believed I would have the money to somehow pay it off.

3. Forgive Yourself

The final step is to write a letter to yourself forgiving yourself for your past financial regrets. Realize that you did the best you could with the knowledge you had at the time. It's part of human nature to make mistakes, and coming to a place of self-forgiveness is symbolic of your personal growth. Remind yourself that you deserve to be forgiven and that you deserve to live a life free of regrets. Whenever you are feeling troubled by negative beliefs about your money situation, take out your forgiveness letter and read it to yourself again.

Part of forgiving yourself also involves learning how to appreciate yourself for who you are. Similar to confidence, self-love doesn't come naturally. It's a skill you learn as you begin prioritizing your personal well-being. Think about the emotional state you were in when you were making all of those bad financial decisions. Did you feel happy about who you were? Were you proud of your financial milestones and where you were in life at the time? When you grow in self-love, it will be a lot harder for you to sabotage yourself by making wrong financial decisions. Instead of being informed by your seeming lack or greed, your self-love will cause you to stop and assess whether the decision is to your benefit and the benefit of your family. Loving who you are allows you to make loving decisions about your finances. Once again, take a moment right now and remind yourself how deserving you are of love. Now make a promise to show yourself the kind of love you deserve!

Exercise: Morning Money Hack Meditation

Researchers say 15 to 20 minutes a day for four days of feeling elevated emotions produce protein to fight bacteria, viruses, and toxins. Imagine shifting your money reality when high emotions are practiced less than 20 minutes a day for 30 days.

The meditation "Mind Hack" by founder Vishen Lakhiani from Mindvalley taught me when we focus on five high-frequency emotions, we tap into money consciousness. I have made some adjustments to fit my needs and call it the "Money Hack Meditation". For best results, this exercise should be performed just upon awakening (during the alpha brainwave stage), before getting out of bed.

Here's an overview:

1. Focus on Compassion for Others (five minutes)— visualize sending compassion to humanity.

2. Focus on Gratitude (five minutes)—imagine one thing in your life you are grateful for.

3. Focus on Love (five minutes)—visualize one thing you love about yourself.

4. Focus on Forgiveness (five minutes)—forgive one person that may have hurt your feelings or forgive yourself if you have hurt someone's feelings.

5. Focus on Your Future (five minutes)—visualize that you have already achieved your money goals or dreams.

Before you can perform this Money Hack Meditation, you must be in a calm and relaxed state. If you can't perform upon awakening, then you can perform a breathing exercise to get you relaxed, have fewer thoughts floating and to accept, believe, and surrender to information without analyzing it.

So, are you ready?

I want you to close your eyes and begin breathing deeply in and out through your nose. Let's repeat this ten times. Just focus only on your breath. If you get distracting thoughts, just let them go and continue to focus on breathing deeply. As you continue to breathe deeply, relax your face, your shoulders, your arms, your fingers, your hips, your upper thigh, your legs, your feet.

Now I want you to visualize a white beam of light above your head. This white light slowly fills your body from head to toe until you're growing as a beam of light. Visualize a beam of light coming from your heart expanding in the room you're in, from the front, left, right, and back of you. Next, expand the light coming from your heart to beam light up to your town, state, country, continent until you beam light to cover the planet. And say, "Today, I send compassion that lives within me to humanity!"

Now, visualize one or two things you're grateful for in your life, whether it's your family or your health. Feel the gratitude from that experience as if it's in the current moment. As soon as you have found the emotions of gratitude, hold it for a few more seconds. If you can't hold on to the experience, just visualize your heart opening and seeing the word or repeating the word "gratitude."

Now, visualize one or two things you love about yourself. Is it your courage, your appearance, intellect, or that you are the bomb-ass momma. Once you have found that experience, feel the emotions of love, and hold it for a few more seconds. If you can't hold on to the experience, just visualize your heart opening, and the word "love" comes out and floats in the air.

Now, visualize one person who may have hurt you or you may have hurt. Once you have found that person, feel the emotion of forgiveness and hold it for a few more seconds. If you can't hold on to the experience, forgive that person and visualize your heart area opening, and the word "forgiveness" comes out and floats in the air.

Now, visualize yourself living the dream of your life. Whether it be a specific goal you want to accomplish, bring your intention from the future into the present moment. Use this opportunity to create relationships, wealth, health, career, or material items. Feel the joy or happiness while you experience the moment.

The more energy you focus on elevated emotions and your future, the more you will leave an energetic imprint in your future reality. The energy imprint will guide your body to this unknown future.

And to make any change in our money reality, there has to be a shift in money consciousness.

Record your results.

Gratitude and Having a Generous Spirit

The Law of Attraction tells us when we focus on what we have and truly feel grateful for it, we will attract more of it. When you are grateful for the job you have, not only will your productivity increase, you will also open yourself to greater opportunities of work. When you are grateful for the income you earn, you attract more money-making ideas or opportunities you come into your life.

Gratitude is powerful because it functions within the abundance mindset. In simple terms, what you see is what you get. If you see plenty, you will attract plenty, whereas if you see lack, you will attract lack. Gratitude can be applied to your finances too. You may not be in the financial position you desire to be in; however, by accepting where you are and genuinely being grateful for what you have and the lifestyle you live, you open yourself to receiving money-making opportunities.

Another spiritual principle that can help you move further along in your wealth building journey is the law of sowing and reaping, taken from the Christian faith. This spiritual law takes on different names in different faiths. For instance, in Hinduism it is known as karma, and in Islam, it is known as Kifarah. The law of sowing and reaping states that whatever you do to others, whether it is good or bad, it will be done to you. If you are unkind toward others, you will reap the same kind of negative response from them. Applying this law to your finances, you can see how damaging it can be to be stingy with your money. Think about it: If you are refusing to share your money with others, how can you expect the Universe to share its wealth with you? By opening your hand in generosity, you are in fact opening your wallet or bank account to receive the abundance the Universe has to offer.

Being humble and having a generous spirit makes you a magnet to wealth. The more you give, the more you receive in return. This doesn't mean you can't draw boundaries with people, especially those who aren't ashamed to take or ask so much of you, without refilling your cup or offering to repay you in the near future. Helping others who are in financial distress or who need access to money urgently is the type of generosity I'm referring to. Although, besides offering money, you can also generously give of your time toward charitable causes, volunteer at a homeless shelter or orphanage, or offer to mentor a young person and transfer your skills to them. All of these forms of giving are equally powerful and can help you attract the financial increase in your life.

Exercise: Gratitude - Reflect On All The Gifts In Your Life

Gratitude is a high vibrational emotion. A powerful energy shift happens when we show appreciation of the simplest and smallest things in our lives. That energy brings in more gifts and presents.

Let's say you worked so hard to give someone a gift, and after receiving the present, they didn't say "thank you." How would you feel? Are you offended, disappointed? Well, that's how the Universe works. The more you give thanks, the more money you will see pouring into your life.

Begin this exercise by listing everything you're grateful for. As you list each one, follow the instruction listed below:

Gratitude List:

1._____

2._____

3._____

4._____

5._____

Instructions:

1. Close your eyes
2. Inhale and exhale deeply twice
3. Smile
4. Say, *"I am grateful for*
   _____*."* or *"I am thankful for*
   _____*."*
5. Keep repeating the phrase *"I am grateful for*_____*."* until you feel the energy expands within you or travels up to the head.
6. Try to hold the feeling of appreciation for at least 15-30 seconds.
7. Repeat steps 1-6 for the next one on the gratitude list.

Chapter 12:

Unconscious Money Resistance

In 2019, I published my first Money Healing Course. In the beginning the enrollment was so slow. I just watched to see how many new enrollments there were, but it was one or two a week. I put in so much importance on the enrollment, I was resisting the success. I was so immersed and entangled in the process, it caused a resistance. As soon as I focused on another project and stopped checking how many enrollments, the number started increasing. The same happened with my ecommerce store. Consistently publishing videos to get online sales, I put too much importance on that one thing. As soon as I focused elsewhere, the sales started coming in.

Have you realized the more desperately you want success, the more scarce it becomes in your life? Have you ever thought about why that happens? Go back to Chapter 1 for a moment and read the discussion we had about money being an energy. Remember how I described money as being an energetic force that enjoys being free to move around and be passed from person to person? When you hoard money or hold on to it tightly, you can repel more of it from coming into your life. Likewise, when you are desperate for money, you give off an aura of lack, and since money is attracted to abundance, you can repel it from coming into your life too.

What I have also found is when you attach a meaning to money, such as money being your source of happiness, you create a resistance to it. The only way you can understand this principle is by putting yourself in the position of money. Pretend you are money and you can freely go to whoever you want and stay for however long you want. If you saw a desperate person who built their whole life on acquiring you, lost friends because of you, and even sacrificed their integrity for you, would you land into their arms?

That would be a huge red flag.

Another red flag would be a person who starts getting physically sick or experiences anxiety when they are running out of money. This type of response toward money can work against them. It reeks of desperation, neediness, and a scarcity mentality. How we handle financial obstacles matters. Making money mistakes cannot be so detrimental to our well-being that we reach the emotional tipping point of anxiety.

We need to learn to see money as being our equal. That's right. Money isn't above us, nor is it beneath us. It is on par with our work ethic, our financial goals, and our purest intentions. When we need money, money comes into our bank accounts, without any questions asked. Why does money respect us so much? Because we respect ourselves and we respect the natural flow of money. When we find ourselves in difficult financial situations, we need to surrender and realize we aren't in control of what happens to us, but at the same time trust that we will be taken care of. The more we chase, the more we will have to fight for money, and I don't think anyone wants to fight their way to $1 million dollars!

The Fear of Failure and Success

What makes you wary of going out of your comfort zone and putting yourself out there? Is it not that you once tried doing that and got hurt in the process? I have often heard people say the best way to teach a child a lesson is to let them fail; once they fail or make a mistake, they will never commit that behavior or action again. There are so many adults who were brought up to fear failing. Failing was considered public humiliation or a sign of weakness and therefore an undesirable experience. Depending on which community you grew up in, you can probably attest to people laughing or mocking those who fail and calling them foolish or naive.

The real fool in my opinion is the "know-it-all" who refuses to try anything beyond their comfort zone. They rely on the limited knowledge they have to judge those who are actually seizing opportunities and learning new skills. These know-it-alls will laugh at those courageous enough to try something and fail, but don't realize that from that experience they have learned valuable lessons that will take them further in life.

Failure is only terrifying to those who believe in their own inadequacies, more than they believe in their own inner strength. If hearing "I can't" feels more true than hearing "I can," it's possible that one will never step out of their familiar surroundings. Changing one's perspective on failure can be useful in making failure less of a hurdle and more of a valuable part of reaching financial success. For instance, instead of someone looking at failure as a sign of weakness, they can see it as necessary feedback about their plans. It's a sign that a few processes or steps need to be reviewed so the plan can become more refined.

The fear of success goes hand-in-hand with the fear of failure. Those who have failed in life fear success because it seems unreachable or they may feel unqualified. The fear of success has a lot to do with having a low sense of self-worth. If experiencing a good life, free of pain and struggle is something that feels awkward, perhaps the problem isn't the goal or desire, but in how one seems themselves. None of us can underestimate how important it is to constantly remind ourselves about how worthy and deserving we are of financial freedom and success. Just because the past is littered with suffering doesn't mean that we were born to live with suffering all of our lives.

Exercise: How to Overcome the Fear of Failure and Success

In this exercise, you will be using a neuro-linguistic programming technique to overcome money fears and anxieties.

You will begin by sitting in a comfortable position without any distractions. Start by taking deep breaths. Breathe in deeply and exhale slowly out. As you exhale, release the stress and tensions. Every time you exhale, relax your muscles as this will calm your nerves.

Repeat inhaling and exhaling deeply ten times. In just one moment, I will be counting down . . . and for each count, I want your relaxation to double.

10 . . . Breathe deeply, and as you exhale, sink in deeper.

9 . . . You are feeling relaxed.

8 . . . Relax and let go.

7 . . . Sink in deeper.

6 . . . Relaxing your muscles.

5 . . . Relaxing your nerves.

4 . . . Relax and let go.

3 . . . Sink in deeper.

2 . . . You are feeling even more relaxed.

1 . . . You are relaxed.

Imagine you are sitting in a chair. It does not matter which type of chair as long you feel comfortable and relaxed.

Think about your money, fears, and anxieties. Now is the time to bring those emotions to the surface of your subconscious mind. Do not resist your feelings. Do not judge any physical sensation. Just know that you are safe.

How are these fears holding you back from your success?

What other emotions do you feel?

Where on your body does it feel the heaviest?

Now create a big ball of light and put all the fears and anxieties you want to let go inside of this ball. Yes, stuff one fear, it could be fear of a debt, bill, criticism or competition inside of this ball because you are ready to wash it away.

Now, imagine the floor opens beneath you, and you sink to the next level into another room. It can be the same or a different room. As you descend, continue holding the big ball of that fear.

As you count down, imagine sinking to the next level for each count. As you sink, the ball of fear and starts to shrink.

10 . . . As you sink to the next level, the ball gets smaller.

9 . . . Sink deeper; the ball is getting smaller.

8 . . . Sink deeper; your fears are washing away.

7 . . . Sink in deeper.

6 . . . All the fears are shrinking,

5 . . . Sink deeper.

4 . . . The ball shrinks to the size of a grapefruit.

3 . . . Sink in deeper.

2 . . . You are letting go of the fears.

1 . . . The ball vanishes.

In a moment, it will be time to come back to your awareness. As you breathe deeply, wiggle your fingers. You are coming back to the present moment. Wiggle your toes as you are slowly coming back. Slightly move your legs. You're coming back to the "now." Slightly move your arms.

Sit for a few moments as you come back to the present moment.

Now you can open your eyes.

Record your results

To access the meditation for this exercise visit: nandaleross.com/mind-your-money-girl-book/.

Exercise: Rewriting the Past

Neil Goddard, one of the pioneers of new thought in the 1950s, created a technique called "Revision." Revision is a technique for rewriting the past. The concept allows one to recall a past event and change the outcome. Rewriting the past helps tear down those barriers of resistance by changing the concept of time to speed up your desire to reality.

The past, present, and future are a sequence of events. According to Einstein, time is just an illusion; past, present, and future exist together. One thing that all change needs is time, "now" and "then."

Using the revision method, I have learned from Jessica Connor, Ph.D. video, you will imagine how much money you desire and what you would be doing with it. It does not matter how real or delusional it might be, but take the time to see it as being real. Immerse yourself in the vision. Feel as if it is your reality.

Now take what has been imagined and placed in your past.

Think of an image in the recent past, such as going shopping or having lunch with the girls or watching the game with the guys at the sports bar, and include that imagined image so that it now reflects that you are receiving this gift you have chosen above. For example, let us say you want to manifest a new job. Recall past events, such as having lunch with friends, and imagine your phone ringing. The company you had an interview a few weeks ago tells you the great news that you got the job. You get excited, and when you get off the phone, you tell your friends the good news. Then envision your friends or family congratulating you.

In other words, use a real-life event that happened in your past and alter the circumstance by incorporating your manifestation coming to fruition. When you incorporate a past event, you can easily remember the feelings that day, the weather, the food you ate, or how a piece of clothing felt against your skin; you are basically using your sensory perceptions.

Continue to vividly remember events that transpired a few weeks ago or a few days ago and incorporate the desired manifestation. Tell the story to yourself and include all your physical senses from that time during this event. This embodies the manifestation.

As you continue to repeat the events, it will create new neural pathways from your past. This technique will remove all resistance of lack or doubt or fakeness because it solidifies your belief that the event has already happened. If you take a desire and place it with a real event, it does not feel like faking it. Because your brain recognizes the past event as true, it acts as if it were real. This is to bridge the gap between your current reality and your altered reality.

As you download the feeling of recalling this event, you will start to raise and alter your vibrational frequency. That calibrates with your altered reality. With practice, your altered vibration will take over as your dominant vibration. This now becomes your dominant frequency. The dominant frequency will become more real to you because you will begin to act, speak, and think accordingly.

The revision method also works wonders when you want to change a negative outcome from a past event. For example, let's say you had lunch with a family member, and they are telling you how you should live your life. They may say "Why would you quit your job. That's a stupid move!" or "Stop dreaming about being rich. It's not going to happen." Yup! The Debbie Downers.

Well, imagine that you got a phone call in the middle of the battlefield. The call is from a company that offered you a high paying position, a salary way more than your family member, Debbie. How would you feel? I'm sure you would love to gloat and brag, but let's stay positive now.

Envision Debbie being happy for you for finding the job. Sometimes when people say "you can't do this or that" or "you don't have the degree to make the money you want," use those words as fuel for your manifestation. Remember, this technique will not change the physical aspect of the past, but it will rewrite your emotions or feelings, moving you closer to your manifestation.

Be creative and try to incorporate the "revision" method in your visualization exercise. You will begin to see an accelerated shift in your manifestation.

Part IV:

Plan for Passive and Multiple

Streams of Income

"Don't chase the money. Even if you want to be a banker. Chase the passion. Chase the dream."

-Tyra Banks

Chapter 13:

Plan to Make Money While You Sleep

I'll share with you one last thing that causes unconscious money resistance, and that is working at something you aren't passionate about. I know that many people are stuck in jobs they don't enjoy because at the moment, putting a plate of food on the table every night is the main goal. I have been there and I understand when earning a salary is far more important than enjoying what you do.

However . . .

If there isn't something you're doing on the side to bring in money so you can one day ditch your current job for the one that is financially fulfilling, you'll be stuck in a never-ending cycle of feeling unsatisfied about your career and where you are in life.

In other words, both of your hands need to be at work at the same time, on different things. One hand is managing your day job (the one you one day hope to leave) and the other hand is managing your passion project or side-hustle (which will hopefully bring you financial success and freedom). Now, if you are fortunate enough to have other hands helping you, you can increase the number of passion projects you're doing, including dipping and dapping in other investments and shortening the time you have to stay in your day job.

Turning Your Passion Into a Passive Income

I've spoken to you a lot about finance and budgeting, but the one financial strategy I haven't spoken to you about is passive income. Passive income is money you make from a side-hustle, which you don't have to actively manage. In essence, passive income businesses run and operate on their own (once you have automated the necessary systems). The benefit of a passive income is that there is no close of business, like traditional brick-and-mortar businesses have. Moreover, if your passive income business is online, you are able to connect with customers from across the world!

I'm purposefully going to talk briefly about passive income because I want you to go and conduct your own research about it once you have completed reading this book. However, I will explain how you can turn your passion into a form of passive income.

Imagine being paid to speak about something you are passionate about or being paid to teach others how to master a skill you are already good at. Does this seem too good to be true? Well, it isn't. There are millions of people who surf the Internet every day to find solutions to their problems. Wherever there are problems, there are businesses seeking to solve those problems. Picture a young single mother who surfs the Internet on how to share her knowledge by creating online courses, publishing books, building a community of fans and marketing tutorials, to showcase her badass momma skills to make extra income for her and her family.

You may be on the other side of the world but have some of the best cooking, parenting, or professional skills your family and friends have ever seen. Perhaps your friends and family have told you many times to pursue a career as a chef, counselor, business adviser, or coach or at least start your own business. Since you have a day job and don't have time to pursue a full-time business, you decide to create a passive stream of income using your knowledge. You access the Internet and create products that you only need to produce once and sell multiple copies over and over again, for a lifetime.

Let's say you decide to create an online course based on your parenting, hobby, arts and craft, career or lifestyle experience, and convert it into a how-to tutorial, podcast, and blog, which you update frequently (and make money from the YouTube, and Google ads you allow to appear on your website or videos). Or, how about converting all your videos and blog content into a paperback and selling on Amazon and many other online bookstore websites? From these three products, which can give you multiple streams of incomes, you could easily make hundreds or even thousands of dollars per month, become an entrepreneur, create your own personal brand, and the best part—leave your day job!

If you don't believe me, once again, I encourage you to go out and conduct your own research (you won't regret it).

Chapter 14:

21-Day Money Guide

Congratulations on reaching the final chapter of the book. Take a moment to connect to your body and sense how you are feeling. Are you feeling overwhelmed with all of the information you have received? Are you feeling energized for the new financial journey ahead? Or are you feeling a little bit sad that the preparation phase is over? If you would love to continue the journey with me, feel free to reach out to me or access some of my additional resources visit: nandaleross.com/mind-your-money-girl-book/.

Before we end off the book, here is a recap of all the necessary steps to take as you prepare to make the money you desire:

STEP 1: Choose (one) of your Dirty Money Secrets or Money Story or Habit

STEP 2: Identify and Release the Money Blockage

STEP 3: Define Your Money Goals and Intention

STEP 4: Rehearse Your Perfect Life

STEP 5: Perform the Money Management Every Month or Every Pay Period

STEP 6: Perform the Morning Hack Meditation Daily

STEP 7: Listen, Write, and Read Positive Money Affirmations

STEP 8: Plan turning your passion into passive income

Conclusion

If someone told me 10 years ago that I would be living the soft life I had always dreamed of in a short period of time, I would've told them to stop playing with me. Back then, I wasn't in the proper mental and emotional space to receive abundance. I thought the world was unfair and no one cared enough to help me succeed. I was surrounded by takers and haters, both of which did very little in helping me stand on my own two feet.

However, deciding to go at it alone, leave my husband and friends who were energy vampires, and close that emotionally taxing part of my life was the best financial decision I could have ever made for my future. Yes, it wasn't easy being a single mother, trying to raise a kid and build a home on a single paycheck. But guess what? The Universe was listening to the silent affirmations I would whisper under my breath. It was paying attention to the silent revolution I was initiating to get my finances back in order.

I desired financial success more than I desired holding on to grudges, falling into the trap of peer pressure, or wanting to prove to others that I was worthy of their love and affection. I was also eager to learn more about money, how it works and moves, and the best ways to attract it. With every good idea I had about my life, I was unknowingly attracting more help and resources from the Universe. The more I desired to improve my life, the better my financial situation got and the wiser I became.

I hope you have truly enjoyed the process of healing your money wounds, money stories, and money blocks. I'm sure there were sections of this book that were difficult to work through. When you are ready, revisit these sections and work through the exercises until you overcome the blocks or emotional resistance. Be patient with your healing journey since most of the beliefs you have released were ingrained in you from childhood. If you feel like the beliefs are slowly creeping back into your life, simply work through the exercises again, until they leave for good.

Once again, I am accessible to you, as a valuable resource you can continue to lean on during your money healing and wealth building journey. If you would like to know more about my money healing course, access more of my resources, or perhaps have a one-on-one session with me, you can reach out to me by visiting: nandaleross.com.

If you have found this book valuable, please may you take a few minutes to write a review.

Monthly Budget Worksheet

For the month of:

PART ONE

DUE DATE	EXPENSES *(Includes car loan, credit cards, student loans, personal loans, household expenses, rent, mortgage, utilities, etc.)*	AMOUNT DUE	BALANCE

	TOTAL EXPENSES		

Add as many rows as you need to list each monthly expense.

PART TWO

ENTERTAINMENT	MONTHLY COST
Alcohol	
Books/Magazines	
Cigarettes/Paraphernalia	
Lottery tickets	
Meals (Dining out	
Taxi/Uber/Lyft	
Beauty services	
TOTAL	

What entertainment cost can you eliminate or reduce to include into your savings?

$_____

PART THREE

INCOME	SAVINGS
MAIN SOURCE: $	STARTING BALANCE: $
OTHER SOURCES: $	CLOSING BALANCE: $

To access the PDF version of this worksheet visit: nandaleross.com/mind-your-money-girl-book/.

References

Block, C. (2011, October 3). *Hoarder or saver? Why you don't let go.* Sane Spaces.

https://sanespaces.com/2011/10/hoarder-or-saver-why-you-dont-let-go/

Collins, M. (2015, April 22). *How to be a conscious spender.* Debt RoundUp.

https://www.debtroundup.com/how-to-be-conscious-spender/#:~:text=According%20to%20Ramit%20Sethi%2C%20a

D, M. (2021, March 8). *Smart budgeting with the 70-20-10 rule.* www.claytonhomes.com.

https://www.claytonhomes.com/studio/smart-
budgeting-a-70-20-10-split/

Dooley, R. (2007, August 24). *This is your brain on money.*
Neuromarketing.
https://www.neurosciencemarketing.com/blog
/articles/this-is-your-brain-on-money.htm

Erb Financial. (2013). *What's your money script?* Erb
Financial. https://erbfinancial.com/whats-your-
money-script/

Fay, B. (2018). *The emotional effects of debt—Denial, stress,
fear, depression.* Debt.org.
https://www.debt.org/advice/emotional-
effects/

Frometa, E. (2021, January 5). *How your confidence is tied to
your money—and how to increase both in 2021.* The
Financial Diet.

https://thefinancialdiet.com/how-your-confidence-is-tied-to-your-money-how-to-increase-both-in-2021/

Gourguechon, P. (2019, February 25). *The psychology of money: What you need to know to have a (relatively) fearless financial life.* Forbes. https://www.forbes.com/sites/prudygourguec hon/2019/02/25/the-psychology-of-money-what-you-need-to-know-to-have-a-relatively-fearless-financial-life/?sh=6c8d8543dfe8

Harris, E. (2017, November 28). *New neuroscience study reveals what worry about money does to your brain.* Forbes. https://www.forbes.com/sites/elizabethharris/ 2017/11/28/new-neuroscience-study-reveals-what-worry-about-money-does-to-your-

brain/?sh=26d0360d385e

Hogan, A. (2020, November 23). *40 Percent of people are keeping financial secrets*. Best Life.

https://bestlifeonline.com/financial-secrets/

Hoobyar, T., Dotz, T., & Sanders, S. (2013). NLP: The essential guide to Neuro-Linguistic Programming. In *Google Books*. HarperCollins.

https://books.google.co.za/books/about/NLP

.html?id=xfB4ipSRAZEC&redir_esc=y

Kaarenperk-vanatoa, K. (2019, May 31). *The 5 triggers of emotional spending (and how to control them!)*. Peachy Loans.

https://www.peachy.co.uk/blog/emotional-

spending/

Kennon, J. (2021, January 20). *A complete beginner's guide to saving money.* The Balance. https://www.thebalance.com/the-complete-beginner-s-guide-to-saving-money-358065

Money is a form of energy. (2013, June 9). News24. https://www.news24.com/news24/MyNews24/Money-is-a-form-of-energy-20130609

Parker, T. (2020, February 15). *How to tell if you're frugal or just cheap.* Investopedia. https://www.investopedia.com/financial-edge/0412/how-to-tell-if-youre-cheap-or-frugal.aspx

Ratliff, K. (2014, June 23). *How to become a conscious spender.* www.jetmag.com. https://www.jetmag.com/life/cents-and-sensibility/become-conscious-spender/

Sawruk, C. (2019, December 12). *Why setting intentions is the way to achieve your goals*. Medium. https://coraliesawruk.medium.com/why-setting-intentions-is-the-way-to-achieve-your-goals-76d5e026d5d5

Sokunbi, B. (2021, January 2). *This is why I'm broke! 5 Money blocks to fix now*. Clever Girl Finance. https://www.clevergirlfinance.com/blog/money-blocks-this-is-why-im-broke/

Valterra, M. (2012, July 9). *5 Steps to healing your financial regrets*. Forbes. https://www.forbes.com/sites/moneywisewomen/2012/07/09/5-steps-to-healing-your-financial-regrets/?sh=5d2a37bf6bf6

Vansomeren, L. (2011, February 13). *How to manage your budget using the 50/30/20 budgeting rule*. The

Balance. https://www.thebalance.com/the-50-30-20-rule-of-thumb-453922

Connor, Ph.D., J. (). *Your Youniverse.* https://www.youtube.com/c/YourYouniverse Channel/videos